Miss Right for Mr. Right

"A Good Man Is
Not Hard to Find."

LEE SPEIGHTS

authorHOUSE®

AuthorHouse™
1663 Liberty Drive
Bloomington, IN 47403
www.authorhouse.com
Phone: 1 (800) 839-8640

KELLY's PHOTOGRAPHY
owned by
Mr. Leander L. Kelly
MS. Rotarsha Kelly

Published by AuthorHouse 12/22/2016

ISBN: 978-1-5246-5656-0 (sc)
ISBN: 978-1-5246-5654-6 (hc)
ISBN: 978-1-5246-5655-3 (e)

Library of Congress Control Number: 2016921115

Print information available on the last page.

This book is printed on acid-free paper.

Chapter 1

The Nature of Women

Not all women are created equal. And I don't mean that on just the superficial, physical level. With due respect to all women, everyone (man or woman) is inherently different, each in his or her own unique way. However, this book is meant to highlight the nature of women in particular. It is out of my utmost regard for women and my deep intent to somehow better understand and relate to you as sensitively as possible that I have decided to research and write about the observable facts surrounding your natures.

The content of this chapter is not mere speculation and definitely not hate-inspired philosophy meant to judge, bash, or criticize women. On the contrary, it consists of actual observations from both personal experiences and collective history and scriptures that I hope will be instrumental in encouraging every man to build deeper, more genuine, and more respectful relationships not only with his girlfriend or wife but also with his mother, sister, and daughter.

We can improve our relationships with others by leaps and bounds if we become encouragers instead of critics.
—Joyce Meyer

To Women

My only wish is for you to open-mindedly bear with me and be able to finish the entire book before forming any premature judgment. I sincerely apologize for any unintentional mistakes and flaws. Please pardon my imperfect yet sincere attempt to somehow share with my fellow men what I have learned about women and how to deal and relate with you.

Again, I wish to emphasize that I have no intent to bash or degrade you. Instead, I hope to improve what little understanding we might have about you so that both men and women alike can positively benefit from a lasting relationship based on mutual understanding, unconditional love, freedom, and respect.

To Men

May this book somehow enlighten you and serve as a helpful guide to making the important women in your lives feel loved, respected, and valued. Your words, actions, and general treatment of women will become one of the most important foundations in keeping your relationships stronger. This book hopes to make you better role models to other people looking for relationships or who are in relationships. In turn, the respect for women will be paid forward to future generations so that relationships can be sweeter and longer lasting.

It is my sincerest wish for my female readers that, after having read this book, you will better understand how to find your Mr. Right or how to be in a position where Mr. Right finds you, how to deal with your man in a way that he appreciates and respects, and more importantly, what the duty of a woman is to her man.

Let's begin with understanding the three personalities of women.

The Three Personalities of Women

I've read in ancient Vedic literature that women can be compared to, if not categorized by, three animal characters. Interestingly, I have found such comparisons quite sound and close to reality. However, they cannot and should never categorize or typecast women. Such personalities can manifest in women singularly or in combinations. Of course, men are not exempted and can also show such characteristics.

1. The Brave and Noble Tigress

A tigress is generally viewed as fierce and brave yet at the same time noble and regal. A woman who is like a tigress is equally fierce in her honesty and frankness, brave in her undertakings, and noble and committed to any task at hand. She is bold enough to speak her mind, follow her own will, and tell you outright if and when she is doubtful of your decision or offended by something you may have unintentionally said or done. A free spirit, she is neither timid nor an introvert.

A Tigress Is Independent

After mating, the male tiger typically leaves the tigress to fend for herself through pregnancy and while raising her cubs. She hunts while she's pregnant and continues to do so after delivery in order to support her newborns. She also has naturally antiseptic saliva for disinfecting wounds. Independent and strong-willed, it is her intrinsic nature to accept life's circumstances as they come.

There are many strong and independent women like this. They continue to face problems head-on, even after experiencing otherwise demoralizing life challenges. These women can survive even without the emotional and physical support of men.

Are You a Tigress?

Did you know that tigers are civilized within their unique circumstances? When many tigers share a single kill, the males often let the females and their cubs feast on the carcass first. Fighting over food is a rare incident with tigers. Instead, they patiently take turns.

So this explains a lot in a relationship. A tigress girlfriend or wife would fare better if men are more like tigers in certain circumstances. In other words, a man who shows some chivalry and gentlemanly behavior may be able to tame the tigress in you and help avoid fights. When there is a misunderstanding, you, the tigress will want to win the argument, especially when you know you are right. You want your needs to come before the man's.

Taming the Tigress

While you are tame and well behaved, you may observe that you are quite fearless, carefree, and independent in the playground. There's simply no stopping you.

In order to be tamed, you need adequate space and freedom. You don't want to feel too confined or controlled. Otherwise, you will rebel.

2. The Gentle Cow

Cows are kind and gentle and have a considerably warm nature. Unless protecting their young, they never attack other living beings, not even stubborn flies. They are tolerant, calmly brushing away insects with their tails and patiently waiting for milkmaids to finish milking. Even their eyes express the same gentleness and kindness. Studies also show that they possess an advanced level of intelligence as well as high emotional sensitivity and complexity. In the company of a cow, a human feels no apparent threat or endangerment.

The Cow—A Symbol of Women's Motherly Nature

In Vedic culture, cows are treated with high respect because they are considered mothers. After all, they provide nourishing milk for us, our children, and our grandchildren. Without milk, we could not enjoy the healthy benefits of butter, yogurt, cheese, and other products derived from it. In many parts of India and other Hindu nations, cows are revered as holy mothers and legally protected. If you kill a cow or act as an accessory to the murder of one, jail time can reach seven years.

Are You the Gentle Woman?

Women who can be compared to cows are slow and gentle, not only in their physical movement but also in their behavior, judgment, and decision making. They are sensitive, smart, kind, patient, understanding, not easily agitated—even when provoked or angered—and often sweet, approachable, comfortable to be around, selfless, and loyal. Unlike the tigress, they are forbearing and don't retaliate unless it's critically necessary. They also have no inclination to engage in a war of words with anyone—or any kind of fight, for that matter. They are softhearted and fragile, and it can truly be heart-wrenching to see them cry as silent tears roll down their cheeks.

This type of woman is quite a rarity nowadays. She simply enjoys being at peace and in harmony with herself and everyone around her. She is admirably simple and practical, clear-headed, honest, and trustworthy, and never picks a fight.

Sensitivity Is Key to Sweeter Relationships

Women who are cows are silent. Similarly, most men are not talkative either. In order to make the relationship and household infinitely better and more peaceful, both parties need to make extra effort in reading between the lines. Be aware of your partner's body language, or better yet, speak up when you need to. You may not be the type to start a fight, and you may want to keep your feelings to yourself, but not saying what needs to be said can make things more complicated.

Air out your feelings instead of letting negative emotions slowly kill your relationship. If you sense that something is out of place, initiating a conversation and asking if something is wrong wouldn't hurt.

3. The Clever Fox

Although women are generally depicted as gentle, caring, and softhearted, they can also be quite cunning. In studying history, reading scripture, and through personal experiences, I've encountered women who are very clever. Unlike the tigress, who openly expresses herself when angry, the fox's mentality and behavior can be tricky and unpredictable. In other words, you can somehow anticipate if a tigress is ready to pounce, but you can't easily predict what a clever fox will do. The following are some examples of women with foxlike behavior.

Cleopatra

You probably are familiar with Cleopatra's story. She was the famous queen and last female pharaoh of ancient Egypt who used her youth, beauty, and charm to the best of her advantage. She seduced, manipulated, and dominated powerful men for the sake of power.

Delilah

Samson, who was a great enemy and threat to the Philistines, fell in love with Delilah, a Philistine girl. When the Philistine rulers found out about this, they convinced Delilah to seduce Samson and trick him into revealing his weakness in exchange for money and, of course, for the safety of her own people. Samson was ultimately stripped of his Herculean strength, blinded, and then enslaved.

Wu Zetian

If you have not heard of Wu Zetian before, she was the *only* empress of China. She started as a teenage concubine and later married the emperor. After her husband's death, she became empress, advocating the elevation of women's social status. She is considered to be the most loved ruler of her time, and her rule filled China with peace and harmony.

The Good, the Bad, and the Ugly

Being clever and smart is an admirable trait in women. However, being sly and manipulative is a totally different thing. I have high respect for women who display quick wit and intelligence, using these to encourage and uplift other people. However, I do have major reservations, doubts, and yes, even fear of women who use their prowess for self-centered reasons.

It can be pretty scary to come across such women who abuse their beauty, charm, and power. To my female readers, please don't be offended and do try to be as objective as possible. In fact, perhaps you have even observed this behavior in yourself. It's not just in the movies or books when sly women wreak havoc in the household and in society. It's surreal yet very real.

How to Deal

If you think you have a tendency to be quite manipulative, my only advice is to be extra vigilant. Of course, don't turn a blind eye to your flaws. It's not only for your sake but also for your man. In the long run, you might end up hurting your relationship and especially yourself. You may not be as submissive as the cow or as fierce and honest as the tigress, but you can be both if you really want to.

To Men and Women

Men, don't typecast all women as sly foxes because they aren't. And women, please don't typecast all men as chauvinists because not all of us are. My point is that we're not static rocks or emotionless robots. Our differences, which will always be there, are what make us unique. There's really no point in bickering and pointing fingers at each other. In a relationship, sometimes men are at fault, and sometimes women are.

What we can try to do, if we're truly sincere in a relationship, is show respect, understanding, and unconditional love for the sake of peace and harmony. Being more understanding and tolerant of each other's weaknesses and boosting each other's strengths, plus lots of respect and love create a more peaceful, happy, and lasting relationship.

Chapter 2

Mr. Right

Every woman has her personal preferences when it comes to Mr. Right. Some would do whatever it takes to get their Mr. Right, right in the palm of their hands. Some would do whatever it takes to capture their Mr. Right. And yes! They would go beyond extreme limits to get him.

Many of you have heard of the saying "beauty comes from within." But let's face it; the very first thing you notice in a person is how he or she looks. This is the initial step of getting that person attracted to you. Although, to get the right man for you, you need to take care of yourself. This becomes so engraved in some women that they make quite an investment in how they look.

Needless to say, to attract Mr. Right, many women spend so much on beauty products that will enhance whatever they have. From a man's perspective, this is not a bad thing because we want our women to always look good. However, to find the right man, some women tend to do some ridiculous things to get noticed.

A lot of women spend so much time reflecting on the clothes they want to wear and the look they want to achieve. They spend a lot of time in front of the mirror, fitting in all the clothes they have to their satisfaction. Some would even go beyond the limits just to be updated with the latest fashion trend.

Some women also go through extreme diets and exercise just to achieve the perfect body that has been engraved in everyone's mind. In a few extreme cases, women turn to surgeries, diet pills, Spanx, corsets, detoxes, and any quick fix or new fad to get their desired bodies. This does not undermine the fact that they can have adverse reactions from doing some of these things, just to attract the ultimate man of their dreams.

But do they really get the right man for themselves? I highly doubt it. Women may be going through these extreme efforts, but superficial things do not go a long way.

Who Is Mr. Right for You?

Generally, there's a certain type of man that a woman wants. A woman looks for certain qualities that have been engraved in her since childhood while looking at her dad and other influences. There may be several ideal types of men, but it is important to make sure that you are suitable for him as well.

1. The Romantic Man

When a man constantly brings you flowers and chocolates and does gestures that make you feel appreciated, he is showing the characteristics of a romantic man. He still keeps the faith of classical romance. A romantic man will look you in the eye and let you know his thoughts. Typically, a woman wants to be acknowledged and appreciated, and a romantic man makes this happen. A romantic man uses intimate gestures to show affection, and as a benefit, you can return the favor by showing him your own romantic impulses.

2. The Self-Assured Man

He is totally confident and secure about himself. A self-assured man can be socially assertive and has a semblance of power and control. He knows his status in a relationship and doesn't feel threatened by other men in a woman's life. A self-assured man doesn't chase for a woman's approval and encourages a woman to feel more confident about herself.

3. The Intelligent Man

The intelligent man initiates intellect-provoking conversations and actively listens to her reply. He can easily make her laugh with his clever sense of humor and exceptional ability to make boring topics seem interesting. The intelligent man may physically change with age, but a woman will be kept interested all throughout the relationship. Intellectual connection plays a vital role in the relationship.

4. The Creative Man

This type of man uses his adroit hands and creative mind to woo a woman. This makes a woman feel special and unique, especially if she is seen as the source of inspiration. Ordinarily, a woman may be fascinated by the way he mixes her into his art. A creative man is instinctive and free-spirited.

5. The Rebellious Man

The rebellious man has a carefree attitude and does not worry about the consequences of his actions. He has a bad-boy image that a woman wants to tame and manage, although she might be futile in her efforts.

Your Definition of a Good Man Depends on Your Criteria

A good man is not hard to find. Whether you want someone who gives you anything you want, someone who will be good to your children, someone who contributes his fair share, or someone who is mentally or physically fit. It all depends on your criteria and your view of a good man.

Generally, an ideal man can't be hard to find if he possesses the certain characteristics that make a good man. A man has to have something that makes a woman feel secure and happy with the relationship. And on the part of the woman, she must also be able to contribute something to the relationship and not depend so much on the man himself. She must also be able to provide assistance and comfort to the man to make the relationship strong.

Moreover, a man must have the character to make a woman happy. This simply means that he must be truthful, honest, and sincere with the woman in order for the relationship to survive. Character is important, as it intrinsically makes a person like something about another person, which bonds the two of them.

Another criterion most women look for in a man is maturity. A woman needs a capable and mature man by her side. She needs a man who is strong enough to solve problems with his own hands, and someone who has dreams and sees where he is going. A woman needs to be assured that she will be taken care of, as a good husband should do.

Intelligence might also be a criterion. Intelligence in a man makes a woman admire and respect him. It also gives security to a woman that he is able to think about consequences. An intelligent man learns to comprehend things before he acts or says anything. This is needed with so many women who want to throw themselves at any married man.

You might also want to look at your compatibility with each other.

This is an element that makes a man and a woman fit well together. Compatibility works like pieces of puzzle, binding you with the common interests you have.

Lastly, but definitely something not to miss, is a man who fears God, for someone who fears God will not be tempted to betray his wife.

Not every man possesses all the qualities I have stated, and it all depends on your criteria.

There are millions of good men out there, but are you willing to make your effort to be qualified for these men?

Why Haven't You Found Your Mr. Right?

If you haven't found the right man for you, it's easy to fall into the trap and ask, "Aren't I enough?" or, "Don't I have the qualities of an interesting person?" or, "Will I ever find the right person who shares the same passion as I do?" Well, certainly that is not true.

It's never a question of who you are personally. It's never about having interesting enough qualities to find the right man. And it is never the case of whether or not you will ever find the man who shares the same passion as you.

There are men out there who are willing to devote and dedicate themselves to you. It is just that these men need your help. And you need to help yourself too. The right man wants you to be the right woman for him too, because he is obliged to take care of you and love you eternally.

You may feel unhappy about still not having met the right person, and you might think that there is a possibility you will never meet Mr. Right and have your ideal happy ending.

You might possibly settle with someone who looks good enough to fill in the intimacy you need. And you might feel inclined to settle for any man who may creates the impression that he will provide you with the intimacy and security you long for—even if he is the wrong man for you.

Maybe you haven't found Mr. Right because you might think that you want a relationship, but beyond that you are more engrossed in living life alone, because it is easier that way. You may be afraid of needing to accommodate the desires and needs of a man.

So listen, what moves a man beyond a woman's beautiful body is her femininity and vulnerability. A man needs these things to compel him to take care of you.

In addition, you have to be equally qualified for the right man. This simply means if you want to have an honest man who won't cheat on you, you have to be honest to yourself too. You have to be honest about your true feelings and not try to conceal them. Or if you want a giving man but you are not eager to give except when he gives to you first, you are not going to meet the right man.

All Men Are Not Created Equal

Some women might say, "Men are all the same." This might be because women typically put men under one category. Men might generally share the same passion for sports, hanging around with friends, or sex among other things, but all men are not created equal.

The generalization mostly comes from the female frustration about men and how they are difficult to understand how a woman feels about a particular circumstance. While men think of emotions in uncomplicated ways, women, on the other hand, are much better in distinguishing their emotional patterns. Women have learned to define their emotions closer to the authenticity of what they feel, while men naturally do not need to do so.

The separation of complex emotional analysis between man and woman is an evolutionary characteristic that has been with us since the beginning of time. Between husband and wife, there basically is an assumption of roles. One takes care of the emotions between them, and the other of the rational strategy of things among them.

This becomes an issue when it comes to gender viewpoint, because on either side there are people who consider this as the case for all of us. They believe that if one character is noticeable, then in some way the other character must be inadequate.

When it comes to relationships, not all men are the same. Most of the problems come when a woman always goes for the same type of man. Men generally differ in most aspects of their lives, although they may share common interests, like most women do. Men vary in their looks, lifestyles, social circles, life goals, intelligence, personalities, and levels of empathy.

A woman needs to know that the diversity of men's characteristics has to do with who she is attracted to. And the complication comes when a woman experiences heartbreak or a certain bad experience from one type of man and then goes for the same type of man again.

Remember that you attract someone who possesses some of the qualities that you want. However, it is important to know that it is about more than the attraction; to get the Mr. Right you are longing for, there should be compatibility and commitment on both sides to achieve the ultimate goal of a healthy relationship.

Chapter 3

A Good Man—Does He Really Exist?

D oes a good man really exist? I say, yes, he does exist, but is he good for you? Are you good for him? You may have even asked, "Why am I always meeting the wrong man?" That's a good question. So this takes me back to what I mentioned in the previous chapter—that your interests are limited to one type of man. You want the type of man you want, but I ask, "Is he really who you need?" Most women who've had bad experiences with men come to the conclusion that there aren't any good men left in the world. I believe that there are good men left. This is a big world.

When your interest, standard, and quality of man that you will deal with remains the same, you'll most likely end up with the same type of man. It all has to do with the law of attraction. You're attracted to someone with qualities that you're fascinated with (i.e., he's tall, and handsome, has a nice body, nice eyes, nice smile, nice hair, or is bald, has money and personality, etc.). This might bring about negative experiences in your life, because you can't see past these qualities to know if he's really a good man.

Most women have a tendency to nitpick every single detail on their grandiose checklist of expectations in men. And this becomes more than just a hindrance. Men are human too. They will not always meet every expectation or standard on your checklist.

You do not have to lower your expectations or standards just to have a man, but men do not have to accept your expectations or standards either. Men sometimes feel insecure and vulnerable just like women do (though we may hide our inner selves). Men want understanding and to be accepted for who they really are as well.

"The steps of a good man are ordered by the Lord, and He delights in his way. Though he falls he shall not be utterly cast down; for the Lord upholds him with His hand" (Psalm 37: 23–24).

What Is a Good Man?

This answer depends on what *your* definition of a good man is. A good man may not be hard to define once you know what you are looking for in your Mr. Right. Knowing what makes you happy is fundamentally the quotient that defines a good man for you. Although men may have their shortcomings, as everyone has, they might find a way to make you feel worth the woman you are.

In most relationships, affection may dwindle at some point in time, but a good man will never cease to make you feel his love for you. A good man will find a way to make you feel wanted, loved, and appreciated. This is a subtle, significant part of keeping the relationship strong. Some men are generally less communicative or affectionate, but be aware of and considerate of the simple efforts he does put forward in the relationship.

Men typically may have difficulty expressing themselves—their fears, emotions, and even their intimate desires—but with the right women, they will open up. So, for a man to be able to be himself, you should also create the atmosphere where he can grow into that comfort. Although a good man may know that some things are better kept private, he will not withhold things from you or suppress his feelings, discerning that this can cause some frustration or tension.

A good man will be honest with you. He knows that this is a foundation of a healthy and happy relationship. A good man knows and understands that keeping secrets will only shroud the relationship into insensibleness. A good man strives to be genuine in all of his ways.

He knows that his actions speak louder than his words; that's why he does little things to make you feel wanted, loved, and appreciated. Mindless of how small those things may seem to him, he recognizes that these are things that matter to you.

A good man also strives to make you feel safe. It is a compliment when a woman tells him how secure she feels with him. Regardless of all those other aspects in your relationship, whether he provides you with all you want and need or how attracted you are to him, when you are able to sleep soundly with your man, these other things do not matter. "In his heart a man plans his course but the Lord determines his steps" (Proverbs 16:9).

Winning a Good Man

Personalities and characteristics have to do with a man's attitude. There may be men who are smitten by their woman with absolute fondness, putting her on a pedestal, treating her like a queen, and putting her happiness above their own. And there are those who come into a relationship acting like the relationship is more of a responsibility.

While it seems there are a majority of men who act more like the latter, it sometimes has to do with how a man sees commitment. Although most men see marriage as an ultimate life goal, it can be like unlocking a combination lock. If the numbers don't align or you don't know the combination, a man might become emotionally secluded and vacant rather than fully committed or energized in a relationship.

Some men might even come up with what I like to call commitment excuses, such as, "I'm just not ready for a relationship right now," or, "I just need space." While these may not be evasion tactics, he may simply believe that you aren't providing the right combination to unlock his lock. When a man says, "I'm not ready for a relationship right now," he's probably saying that he's not ready for a relationship with you.

When a good man finally meets that woman with the right combination to unlock his commitment lock, he perseveres to get her. He will hang on and commit because he will not want to take the risk of losing her.

Commitment is not some sort of an aversion within men, but in order to get the number sequence right to crack that commitment lock, you have to be the right woman for him, too. If you want to win a good man's heart, you have to understand what it takes to bring about the right kind of reciprocity. You have to know what it is that makes a man want, in order for him to make a commitment to you.

Be Willing to Sacrifice

Relationships change over time, and struggles are like roller coasters (i.e., they go up, they go down, they go fast, they go slow, they stop, etc.). At some point in your life, you have to take the steps to keep the relationship moving forward. Some women are just there when things are going well, and some disappear when things go badly. I don't just mean literally disappear or leave but mentally and emotionally as well. Meaning, their bodies are still there, but their minds and hearts are no longer invested in staying in the relationship. Some women are just willing to take credit for the positive, and when the relationship turns bad, it's the man's fault, and he's left with the negative.

Being in a relationship is hard work and requires a lot of sacrifices. When something goes terribly wrong, it's not right to put blame on each other, and it is not right to leave your man behind. An example is when a man is having a hard time with his finances and is not making enough money to provide for his woman, family, or himself.

A good relationship is about more than what one party is getting out of it. It's what you do in it together. You have to instill in yourself that being with the right man isn't just all about the fun times, but more than anything else, it is being there to make and endure sacrifices life throws at the both of you.

Relationships may not be easy, but if you are willing to make it work, your man will definitely make it work too. If you put effort into the commitment, men will put in as much effort as you do. It's a two-way process wherein you both have to put in the needed effort for each other.

If you love someone; is there really a right time to let go of the love if it's still there? If that man means something to you, there is always the right reason to fight through whatever stands in your way. You should be prepared to do whatever it takes to keep him in your life. After all, no one ever said that finding the right man would be a walk in the park. It can take a lot of hard work, not just on your part but on his too.

Be Equally Qualified for Your Man

Most women want to have the right man for themselves without considering whether they are right for him. To get and to keep Mr. Right, you must be equally qualified for him. This is what a lot of women fail to realize. You want a man if he's got money, a nice car, a nice body, a nice home, a job, or whatever it is that intrigues you. Do you have these things or qualities yourself?

The right man comes along for some women, but they do not match the same attitude or characteristics. You might be smart, strong, and successful and want a man to be smarter, stronger, and more successful than you or at least come close to the level that you consider yourself to be on. You may be meeting on some levels, but it does not mean he is equally qualified for you.

Just think of the cliché, "Opposites attract!" Generally, men with those mentioned traits may be looking for women who are less busy, more free, less demanding, and lower maintenance. So what happens when both of you are on the same level with the same type of characteristics?

What happens when you get with an equally driven and busy man? Both of you are used to getting your way and are not big on compromise. Now there's friction between you. In general, men look for women who would make their lives better simply by being optimistic—not someone who can or always wants to beat him at what he does. A man looks for a woman who can offer an appreciative feminine energy to his masculine energy.

So if you are a woman who does not consider yourself as a hard-driven, powerful CEO type, it might be effortless for you to have one of these types of men, because you offer something that a successful man or a not so successful man wants. You're someone who has more time to devote to him.

Most men generally want a woman who is nurturing, thoughtful, supportive, understanding, honest, fun, and free-spirited. A man simply wants someone who will complement his other characteristics or fill in the gaps of his weaknesses.

If you constantly assume that the more impressive you are, the more it's going to grant you with an impressive man, think again. Men don't need to be challenged or criticized in this area. Now, this does not mean that men may be turned off or intimidated; they simply want to turn off their hectic outside world and go home to a mellow home.

Be Ready to Fill in the Gaps of His Weaknesses

Men typically have been instilled with the genetic code to be the breadwinner and the defender and to have that single-minded attitude of doing things for themselves without any help. When a man is in a dilemma, he tends to shut down. This is what women sometimes do not understand. Coupled with a man's inability to sometime communicate his emotions well, women often see this as a problem. Understand what your man is going through and be there to support him.

More than anything else in this world, more than money, love, sex, more than power, pleasure, or fulfillment, we are all stimulated to seek validation—the feeling that we deserve acceptance, that our thinking and opinions align with others, and the guarantee of knowing that there's a place where we are recognized.

Validation can be a very powerful human desire that guides us to form valuable relationships. Women want and need certain validations from a man, but men also want and need certain validations from women.

In addition, a woman must be ready to fill in the gap of a man's weaknesses. You should fully understand what your man is capable of and discern where he is lagging. This is where you take your space in a man's life to make him incessantly captivated and devoted to you. He needs to know that you will be there for him instead of tearing him down or belittling him.

When a man sees that you fill in where he has certain flaws, he will be more dedicated to keeping you and keeping the relationship going strong. This is one way to keep the right man in your life. Men may be or become weak in some areas of their lives, but I believe they can rebuild as long as you're helping to fill those gaps.

Share the Responsibility in the Process of Decision Making

I think for the most part, there should be an equal share of decision making in the relationship. Not only does this open up the communication experience among the couple, but it also builds trust and optimism.

Well-balanced decision making can be like driving down a winding road. There are brisk turns and speed bumps where you both have to decelerate so you don't end up crashing. Those speed bumps represent the decisions you create together, and the road represents your relationship.

This can be different when you are single. The road can be tranquil without any bounces. Your life can be simple, like a highway where you feel that you can ride all you want. When you get into a relationship, you have to share the responsibility of decision making. Now you have to slow down for the brisk turns and bumps, because it's no longer just you.

Sharing the decision-making process makes it easier for both of you to live a better life together. Taking in different sides of the story helps you to understand the whole picture better. And not only that, it gives you opportunity to see each other's side and how you can relate to each other better. Sharing the responsibility in the process of decision making also helps to create a relationship that is built on reliance.

So if you ever find yourself arguing with your man about mundane things like how much to spend on a gift or what silverware to buy, it should not create a major predicament between the two of you. It's natural to get into arguments. Talk to and listen to each other; then make the best decision for the both of you.

Strive for Perfection but Don't Expect Your Man to Be Perfect

The perfect man does not exist. All women should know that. Although it's normal for women to strive for perfection themselves, what they should rather consider is, is he the perfect match for them? That is the key element that women should be asking, not about the perfection of a man but about how perfectly they're matched.

Every man has his flaws. He may not be that tall, dark, handsome man of your dreams, or perhaps he leaves his dirty clothes laying around. At no time will you ever meet a man who does not have flaws. However, as long as those flaws are not considerable setbacks, it's always acceptable to give him a chance. Who knows? You might even get the hang of his flaws. Take into consideration that you are not perfect either. Even if you are a perfectionist, you still have your own flaws. This is what makes you different. If you are not perfect, why should you be with a perfect man?

So, although you might be attracted to some physical attributes that may seem like perfection to you, if you consider time and age, you are going to see him develop graying or balding hair, or maybe a big belly. This just goes to show that your classification of perfection doesn't last forever.

You should know that Mr. Right for you is simply imperfectly perfect. The right man for you is human, and you should know if he's compatible with you. You may learn to love his flaws and end up seeing him as the ideal man for you.

See the Goodness in Your Man

When a woman experiences problems, she often talks about it to the person closest to her. It might be her mom, her father, her best friend, her pastor, or even a person unrelated who has no affiliation to her. A woman finds ways to discuss her problems so it's easier for her to cope with them. A man, however, tends to drown his problems out by sulking in silence or lying in front of the television. This makes him tranquil as he starts looking for solutions to his problem. And a man would usually do this on his own, without the help of anyone. When a woman approaches him with a suggestion or advice, a man may typically be annoyed.

Men also interpret feelings differently than women do. Women are more receptive to visual, verbal, and other types of signals people provide. For example, when a woman walks into a crowded room, she visually scans for people, noticing who gets along well with whom and who is in a good mood. Similarly, most men walk into a room full of unfamiliar people and look for familiar faces, where the exit areas are, and possible threats. Nonetheless, men typically do not comprehend when a woman feels upset unless she directly discloses it to him. Normally, a woman would expect a man to read the indirect signals she's throwing out instead.

Men have a way of seeing things from a different perspective, and a woman needs to understand this. He deals with solutions to problems rather than the emotional aspect of it. Men also deal with tasks differently than women do, and they may want to deal with a single task at a given time. This has to do with the evolutionary way we have unfolded, as men needed to concentrate on hunting for food. Women, on the other hand, revolutionized to forage for food, tend to the children, and perform different tasks all at once.

Men and women may be different in several ways, but you should always see the goodness in your man. Seeing the goodness in your man, regardless of the things he does, allows you to fully understand him and nurture the good side of him.

Allow the Man to Be a Man

A good husband makes a good wife. And when a man makes a woman feel good about herself, she can definitely reciprocate much better. So to make your relationship much better, allow your man to be the man he is. Now, this does not mean you have to condone the wrong he does, but on a stricter sense, you should always give him the space he needs in the relationship as well as the benefit of the doubt.

Allow the man to be reliable, supportive, and responsible in the relationship. Every woman wants and needs a reliable man. A woman needs support in some phases of her life, so let him support you in the way that he can. However, do not be dependent in every way, for a man also wants a woman to be self-reliant in some ways. He can be your shoulder to cry on if you need, but be independent in certain ways so as not to be a burden.

When the right man comes into your life, allow him to be the man that he is and never force him to be or do what he is not. Simply, the right man will do the right things that you expect him to do.

Chapter 4

The Dos and Don'ts When You Meet a Good Man

Knowing who the right man for you is and knowing the rights and wrongs when keeping that man is crucial for the relationship to withstand the tests of time. More importantly, being the woman you are for a particular man is part of the foundation that connects the two of you.

It is important to know your man well enough to judge what he likes and dislikes. As with every relationship, both have to adjust to each other's wants and needs in order to have balance. Ultimately, if a man fails at something, it is the woman's duty to fill in the gap so that the relationship becomes whole, as mentioned earlier.

When you meet Mr. Right, you have to be Ms. Right yourself. Finding the right man will not change you into the preferable person that he is looking for. If you are lazy and self-absorbed, meeting an unselfish and diligent man will not change you. If you are an uninteresting and shallow person, finding an intellectually stimulating man is not going to alter who you are.

Rather, you should learn to be interesting, kind, caring, and selfless. Maybe fashion yourself after women you respect and work hard to improve your character flaws. Also work hard to become a well-rounded woman. Learn things that will make you more complete. For example, engage yourself in volunteer work, such as working with less fortunate people, which will probably help you learn the value of humility. Seek professional advice if you need to learn how to be self-assured or if you have childhood traumas that may be blocking you from pursuing and living a happy life.

Simple things that will make you happy will ultimately be valuable not only for yourself but also when the right man comes along. So be happy in the real sense of the word. No matter how perfect your Mr. Right is, and even if he has all the means to make you happy, he will not help you become satisfied if you are not already content within.

Your happiness in the relationship will be a reflection of how you feel inside.

Cheating

There might be differences in men and women and the reasons why they tend to seek infidelity. It is said that men generally look for more physical attention while women seek to fill an emotional void. In my opinion, women who are satisfied with their relationship are not likely to cheat. I believe there is a greater percentage of single women who have done so at a specific time in their life. Some women look for perfection in their men, and when this perfection is not found or is no longer there, they look for it in other men.

The reasons for cheating can be as shallow as a woman thinking that what she has is a dashingly gorgeous man on her arms, but she dumps him because he does not have enough money to fill her desires. Then she goes on to another man, looking for him to pick up the slack. If she cannot find or get what she is looking for, then she moves on to another one.

Now, moral standards come into question. If you want a good man, you must be content with the qualities he embodies. More than that, if your man no longer displays the qualities that initially attracted you, you may want to reexamine the relationship. I say reexamine because in your eyes the future of the relationship may be in jeopardy. In his eyes, he may believe the relationship is just fine. Remember, he is not perfect. If you always look for what you consider to be the perfect man, you will never be satisfied with whoever comes along in your life. So take a moment to have a conversation with your man.

Exploiting

Men are generally exploited in an understated and subtle way. And while feminists may argue that in a conventional relationship, women are the ones who are exploited, men are usually the target of exploitation. Nonetheless, there are women who exploit their men in a more discreet manner that is indistinguishable to men.

Some women are much more intuitive than men in a sense, and they know exactly what is happening. This becomes a problem because some men are blind toward understanding a woman's behavior.

There is a saying that goes, "Give them an inch, and they'll take a mile." This can be true, especially when a man has a hard time setting his personal boundaries. The dynamics at play in a relationship have something to do with men being exploited. Moreover, there are women who exploit and walk over men just so they get the benefit of simply having them there to do what they want and to provide the things they want.

Women, especially those who are at the top of their game, will tailor their behavior depending on the man they are with. This simply means if a man has strong personal boundaries and high standards, a woman will tune her character to be at her best behavior and extremely nice.

However, with a more provider type of man who does not have a strong sense of reality and is not very confident, she'll behave unrulier, simply because he allows her to. Take for example if they go out to dinner and the man insists that he'll pay, she will allow him to. Or if she is grumpy and pushes him around, he'll simply allow her to do those things. He will let this type of behavior go just to keep the peace, or he'll think that if he does not get her the things that she wants and if he doesn't let her have her way, she'll leave.

If this type of woman sees that the stream of benefits has dried up, she'll probably leave him anyway. She continues to enjoy all the gifts, dinners, and everything else that comes along with this man but finds nothing else fascinating about him. Some women have some men friend-zoned, just so they can still get what they want while leaving him hanging.

Mistreatment

Have you ever considered that your attitude might be a form of mistreatment when it comes to your man? Women sometimes have an attitude that's so bad it's almost a form of mistreatment. Believe it or not, this happens. The conventional abusive relationship is that of a man physically abusing a woman, but men are oftentimes on the receiving end of a verbal, emotional, and sometimes physical abusive relationship as well.

There are various terms used to describe a behavior like this—pushy, demanding, harsh, argumentative, nagging, aggressive, obsessive, and even passionate. And this can be followed with excuses like, "She had a bad childhood experience. She was taken advantage of." There are women who have less quintessential beginnings but don't bring that past into their adult relationship.

Men are generally persuaded to believe that this is normal for women, especially because women are seen to be unreasonable, moody, sensitive, and demanding. Most men will accept this kind of behavior, thinking that this demeanor is just how she expresses her feelings. This is outrageous because this kind of attitude thrown toward a man makes him uncomfortable, just as a woman who was a recipient of it would be.

You need to put a stop to this kind of behavior. If you flip out over a man's petty wrongdoing, simply because you are not in the mood, this is emotional mistreatment. Emotional abuse can be like cancer that hoards the mind until he is left feeling incapable and worthless. You may not notice it, and you may not be abusive as you perceive it, and sometimes you might be nice and even make loving gestures.

Ask yourself this: Is everything that happens in your life his fault? Do you always look for ways to manipulate him in order to get what you want? Is he spending more time at work than with you? Has he backed away from his friends and family?

A good man may not let you know what he feels inside, but if you constantly keep this kind of behavior, there will be a greater chance for the relationship not to work. A man needs to feel like he is the man in the relationship, and you, as his woman, should reaffirm that to him.

Neglect

Some women forget the need to encourage their men. They do not realize the negative effects of neglecting and not encouraging their men. Encouraging your man will ultimately build or reassure his self-esteem and lift him up to conquer the world.

A man who lacks encouragement from his woman will be worn down and not accomplish any great task he has at hand. You should know a man needs uplifting from the woman in his life. There is a saying that goes, "Behind every great man is a woman." A man needs a woman to be his cheerleader, someone who encourages him in everything that he does. Someone who believes in him, whatever the hurdles may be.

It can be a total disaster for a relationship if the woman does not encourage her man when he tries to better himself. If you want your man to conquer the world, be there for him and do not fail to always encourage him. Make him feel that he can do well.

Some men feel down or like less of a man because they lack encouragement. If you want your man to be the man you want him to be, encourage him. For a man needs a woman to make him feel strong. Eventually, if you do not encourage your man, he will only see himself as someone who provides, and he will not expect anything from you. Sooner or later, he may look for that in another woman.

Some women expect love from a man without reciprocating the gesture with good things. A man also needs love, and more than that, he needs to feel encouraged to do better. So the question is, what seeds are you planting? What are you doing to make him feel your love? For there are other ways to show love instead of sex.

So to keep the right man in your life, it is important to always encourage him. Lift him up. Say, "You're going to make it." Say you're with him every step of the way. Make your man feel confident about himself, because a man who receives encouragement from his woman can conquer the world. Be his support and his cheerleader.

Trust Issues

Trust can be the most relevant ingredient in building a strong relationship. Trust can be earned, learned, and nurtured, provided you both work on cultivating it. Trust issues can also be a major problem in a relationship. It may not be the number-one problem, but it definitely is a leading cause of many breakups.

In every relationship, it is important to know that trust is earned and not given freely. In such conditions as a romantic relationship, trust is earned. So do not feel bad about demanding character and loyalty.

Trust issues become a problem when you enter into a new relationship and you bring unsettled problems from a past relationship. This becomes an detrimental problem because you obstruct the new man from giving you his all. And you do not give him a fair chance to do so. The pains you encounter and the unresolved issues can ultimately spill into the relationships that follow. This spill can be a major issue and lead you to destroy the new relationship.

Nonetheless, a relationship where there is no trust can be abusive—verbally and physically. So in every relationship, it is important to create a safe emotional space. To create one, you need to continuously work to improve your communication skills.

It is good to cultivate and develop good listening skills, as this can be the hardest to establish. Learn to fully understand what each of you is saying. It is also important to express your needs clearly and assertively. Not being able to express your needs can lead to a breakdown of trust. When a man and a woman are able to direct and meet each other's needs constantly, it is the most impressive way of building a trusting relationship.

Another thing to consider is not allowing things to get resolved. When a couple does not get issues resolved within themselves, resentment develops, and trust becomes adrift. This becomes a root cause of so many breakups and heartaches. When you meet the right man for you, make sure that both of you learn to work on your problems or issues together.

Chapter 5

Men and Women

There might be a difference of opinion when it comes to the behavior in a man and a woman's relationship, and this may be due to the difference in gender. But how do they really behave in a relationship, and what are the myths when it comes to a romantic relationship? Generally, men and women are more similar than we think, and our typical presumptions are incorrect.

Firstly, it may be hard to accept, but men can be as romantic as women, if not more romantic in some cases. Although most romantic movies and contemporary writings are fashioned toward the female audience, some men have a romantic perspective on love as well. Men are also inclined to believe in the romantic concept of love at first sight.

Admitting the physical attractiveness in a potential mate is far more important to men than women. There is actually a study where college students were asked to rate the importance of physical attractiveness prior to selecting their date. Women rated physical attractiveness far lower than men did. However, when it came to the speed date itself, the discrepancy disappeared. So regardless of what the initial data showed, both men and women favored physical attractiveness in their potential partner. There may be a small difference, as men value it more, though the difference may not be far off.

Also, it might not be socially common for women to accept casual sex, but in reality, men tend to blow out of proportion the number of partners they've had, and women tend to depreciate the number of partners they've had. For women to be open to casual sex, the situation has to be right. This does not mean that women are not roused, but women are more particular about whom they prefer. This occurrence is likely to happen in the situations of occasional dating relationships, friendships, and hookups.

In terms of handling conflict, there is a study that men and women do not contrast very much. A couple might be hooked where one argues about an issue and the other withdraws to avoid the argument. More commonly, the one who pushes for an issue is the woman, and the man withdraws from the discussion. This becomes a vicious cycle where both become frustrated. Traditionally, men hold more power in the relationship than women do, so women are more likely to find themselves insistent on change. Men, on the other hand, simply want to continue the situation.

Double Standards

The world has revolved around expectations from one another that do not have any sensibility. So regardless if it originates in our own self-doubt or some ingrained thirst to berate each other, we're critical of calling out someone who does not meet or exceed our measures.

Men and women have quite a few principles that are unfairly adopted in a contrasting way. Sometimes this has to do with how society has developed its ideas of how a man and woman should act in the eyes of everyone.

Double standards between men and women should not exist, but they do. You shouldn't expect something of your mate that you're not willing to do or not do yourself. You shouldn't want to be treated a certain way when you're not willing to provide that same treatment.

"Do to others as you would have them do to you" (Luke 6:31).

The Differences between Men and Women

Men and women may have varying views about relationships, and the old quote, "men are from Mars, and women are from Venus" only limits the discussion about it and gender differences. It stresses the perception that gender is black and white, and people are ascribed to a certain set of preferences with their gender.

When it comes to ending relationships, most people who break up have one general reason—their most important needs were not understood or met. In most relationships, people are more often interested in having their own needs met, and they fail to consider the particular needs of their partners. And the problem with addressing the unique needs between men and women becomes more significant when it comes to their differences.

In essence, both men and women have the same primary needs—to be loved, to be noticed, and to have a purpose in the relationship. Still, it's how men and women devote themselves to having those needs met that creates the necessary differences.

Both men and women have the need to be loved and cared for, though they may act on it differently. For instance, some men do not talk about their emotions and loving feelings openly, while most women tend to share their feelings openly. While most women would want to have their men express their emotions to them, women should simply understand that some men would rather show their love through actions and not words. A man might take you out to dinner or buy you a special gift as a way of showing affection because some men believe that actions are better than words.

Also, both men and women have the need to be noticed by their partners. When a man is having a bad day, he needs his mate to understand that he is having a bad day, and this can be done simply by inquiring if he is okay. In most cases, some men would just grunt a few immediate words about their bad day and move on. On the other hand, most women want to talk about their bad day in detail. This need can be one of the most significant needs in a relationship, and if it is not met, a person may feel depressed, angry, and neglected, and it may even lead to those needs being fulfilled elsewhere.

The Similarities

Men and women have similarities in their desires. These desires all come down to four areas in our life, emotional, physical, sexual, and spiritual. If we are not paying attention to these important areas in our lives, letting the relevant God-created process fill our desires, we will pursue improper means to fill those deprivations.

With the emotional aspect of our lives, men and women hunger for three things—the need to be heard, to be affirmed, and to be accepted for who they are. It might be common to hear couples grumble that their partner is not listening to them when they are having a problem. When people do not feel understood, they might carry out their desire to feel heard by raising their voice or having an outbreak of temper.

The emotional hunger to be affirmed for our efforts is commonly the desire to understand that our actions are acknowledged. Affirming what our partner has done for us can be crucial to let them know that we recognize the effort and time they spend to care for us. In addition, being accepted for who we are and what we can offer in the relationship is important. If we let our partner know how important they are in our lives simply because they exist, not always because of what they do or do not do but because of who they are, it will create tranquility in a troubled relationship because it encompasses long distances.

Physically, both men and women have a desire to feel safe and to be touched. We need to feel secure in our lives and especially in our relationships. When one is secure in a relationship, he or she is more open to communication and much more inclined to engage in deeper intimacy. The desire to be touched is an important aspect in our lives. Men and women feel the need to be wanted by their partner.

Touching is a form of communication. It's important to let your partner know you notice him and appreciate the time spent in his company. This can be as simple as you throwing your leg over his leg while sitting at home watching television or by laying your head on his shoulder. Don't let tender moments pass. This can be the same for men and women—the wonderful feeling of simple gestures of acknowledgment from each other.

Lastly, the spiritual need of both men and women is something that keeps them bonded together. When the spirituality of the man and woman is forsaken, they often find themselves abandoned and lonely, as there is a spiritual void that forms within them.

Though men and women have differences in some aspects of their lives, there are more similarities in the fundamental facets in life. And to create a meaningful relationship, this should be addressed and approached carefully.

Chapter 6

Submission

It's not enough to aspire for a long-term and lasting relationship; you should aspire for a relationship that is as sweet and peaceful as it is lasting. There are relationships that can last for decades till death does its eternal job of parting couples. However, not all lifelong partnerships are actually pleasant or fulfilling. You sometimes see this in elderly couples who never stop bickering over the littlest of things.

Sure, they may have built their reputation within their social circle for having reached the rare silver wedding anniversary. They may even have reached their golden or diamond anniversary, which can be quite impressive considering this modern age of infidelity and divorce. Yet these external milestones do not automatically mean that a marriage is, in fact, a true success.

This can be compared to the natural human desire for health and longevity. There's certainly nothing wrong with wanting to age gracefully. On the other hand, living a fuller and more meaningful life holds greater significance than living a long but discontented life.

In other words, longevity is not necessarily equal to life fulfillment and satisfaction. You can live to be ninety but still feel unaccomplished.

Your relationship may last an entire lifetime, but you may feel unfulfilled and unhappy throughout.

So how can you get the best of both worlds? How can you build an equally fulfilling and lasting relationship? It's through love-based submissiveness. Hopefully, the following jewels of wisdom can somehow enlighten you and uplift your relationship to a deeper, sweeter, more satisfying, and more meaningful platform that is beyond all physical considerations and boundaries.

In a Relationship of Love, There Should Be Yin and Yang

For a relationship to be peaceful, nourishing, and lasting, there should be constant equilibrium and harmony. Otherwise, it will simply end up being chaotic, destructive, and agonizing. This balance can be maintained by submissiveness from both parties. Sometimes, you're right, and he's wrong. Sometimes, he's right, and you're wrong.

Now when both of you are right, sometimes you should submit and have it his way, and sometimes he should let you have it your way. A relationship wherein only one person is the dominant one, and the other is always the submissive one is not a healthy and balanced one.

Let me give an analogy. In order for a seesaw to work, two people must patiently take turns boosting each other up. Otherwise, one side will always stay up, and the other will always stay down. The seesaw won't function as it should. It'll be stuck, and that's no fun at all! In fact, this defeats the purpose of riding a seesaw. Ultimately, you simply want to get off the seesaw.

A relationship is somewhat like this. For it to work, you should accept the inevitable fact that you're not always up. There will be circumstances when you have to stay down and close to the ground in order to boost your partner up.

This is selfless and submissive love. It means being humble enough to accept being on the lower end of the seesaw from time to time, just to see your partner up. If your partner feels the same way about you, he will do the same. He will also humbly and willingly stay grounded to be able to lift *you* up.

With this attitude of loving submissiveness, relationships get infinitely better. As long as there's love and respect for each other, there's no need to fight over petty things.

"There is nothing nobler or more admirable than when two people who see eye to eye keep house as man and wife, confounding their enemies and delighting their friends," Homer said.

Submission—Real versus False

Most women fight tooth and nail against the idea of being submissive, perhaps due to common misconceptions surrounding the term. So what does it really mean to be submissive? Here are a few quotes to hopefully shed light on the subject.

"Submission is not about authority and it is not obedience;
it is all about relationships of love and respect."
—William Paul Young, *The Shack*

Paul Young truly knows his stuff. And he definitely practiced what he preached. He remains happily married, with six children and eight grandchildren. Truly, it's all about love and respect.

For instance, it wouldn't hurt if you submit to your man by making him coffee every morning, if you know that he likes it. Sure, he can do this little task himself, but men like feeling loved and cared for. And this is why you are in a relationship—to love and care for someone, and to be loved back and cared for by that someone. Being in a couple should not be a battle of the egos about who's higher or lower. It's supposed to be a mutually loving situation wherein both work together in peace and unity for a common goal.

Unfortunately, most married couples nowadays are no longer bound by one common goal. In fact, each has his or her own ulterior motive. The usual scenario is that the man wants to be master of the household. The problem is that the wife also wants to be master. Since neither one wants to submit to the other, out of selfishness, ego, and pride, they ultimately decide to go their separate ways.

> "It is not a lack of love, but a lack of friendship
> that makes unhappy marriages."
> —Friedrich Nietzsche, 1800s German philosopher

So how do you keep harmony in your relationship? It's by making a sincere and conscientious effort to cast aside all pride, ego, and self-interest. Lock these up in a heavy wooden trunk and throw it into the abyss. And don't forget to get rid of the key. Of course, this can be very difficult since self-centeredness and self-preservation are intrinsic in us humans. Yet it is made possible with the help of another intrinsic trait—love. Not to be melodramatic but allow me to say this trite expression: love conquers all. Love conquers your own selfishness. Truly, the more you love, the more selfless you become.

A loving mother puts her children's needs and comfort over hers. Before she got married and had children, the center of her life was herself. When she got married, the center of her life became her marriage. And when she had kids, the scope of this center shifted to the entire family as a whole, getting wider and wider. This is true submission. Yes, it is selfless and sometimes difficult. Yet it is voluntary and done out of love.

> "To be feminist doesn't mean you can't be submissive."
> —Sam Taylor-Johnson

False submission, on the other hand, is one that sprouts from fear and sheer force or coercion. This poor and perverted reflection of the real thing is what you usually see in battered wives and girlfriends. Unfortunately, this is what generally passes as submission, thus irking feminists. Let me say this once again. That is not submission in the truest sense of the word. That is simply coercion.

When you submit, you are not doing so as a slave who is forced. You willingly consent. You love and respect your man, and so you submit to him, knowing full well, of course, that he also has the same love and respect for you. In other words, you know that he would do the same. You want to give him the last slice of pizza because you know that he'd do the same for you and not out of fear that he will get mad or hit you. You submit and let him win an argument because you know that he's right and you're wrong in that specific circumstance.

Here's a biblical verse emphasizing this need for love and respect as the basis for submission.

"Submit to one another out of reverence for Christ. Wives, submit yourselves to your own husbands as you do to the Lord. Husbands, love your wives, just as Christ loved the church and gave himself up for her. Each one of you also must love his wife as he loves himself, and the wife must respect her husband."
—Paul the apostle, Ephesians 5

Inseparable from love and respect are humility, patience, and kindness. With the presence of these qualities, the home becomes a place of peace and harmony. Another verse from the Bible immediately comes into mind.

"Love is patient, love is kind. It does not envy, it does not boast, it is not proud. It does not dishonor others, it is not self-seeking,

it is not easily angered, it keeps no record of wrongs. Love
does not delight in evil but rejoices with the truth. It always
protects, always trusts, always hopes, always perseveres."
—1 Corinthians 13:4–7

The Art of Submission—When to Submit and When to Step Back

After having differentiated between true submission and false so-
called submission, I believe it would be wise to expound that even true
submission has its drawbacks. While being stubborn only makes things
worse, being too submissive is equally destructive. Being submissive
when called for is definitely beneficial to your relationship. Following
blindly and gullibly is definitely not.

When your man is right and you know it, then it doesn't hurt to
be submissive. But if he's wrong and you know it, then it's not the right
time to submit. Knowing when to submit and when to step back is an
art that requires a little objectivity and a lot of sensitivity—the former
for distinguishing right from wrong, and the latter for respectfully
disagreeing without being offensive.

Being objective is required in order to actually determine who's
right. Without it, you can't really tell who's right and who's wrong,
especially while in the heat of an argument. You have to try to step
back and be objective enough to discern whether you are actually right
or only *think* that you're right. If you're wrong, then humbly submit. It
can be tough, but it's definitely worth it. It'll spare you from constantly
bickering over petty things.

Now, if you objectively and sincerely think that he's in the wrong,
then you must say so but with all respect and humility, and without
arrogance or conceit. After all, you can't just submit to and follow what
you think is not right. Yet you shouldn't start a war knowing that you
could prevent it. In other words, be gentle and sensitive in your words

and actions even though you know in your heart that you are right. You have to spill the beans, but do it gently. Otherwise it will be messy.

Being in a relationship is like dancing. It can be difficult to dance with two left feet. But with time, patience, determination, and a sense of humility, you can learn. Now if your dance partner is the one with two left feet, be patient and understanding enough to teach him. Otherwise, the dance will simply end up disastrous. It takes two to tango, so both of you should learn the basics.

Chapter 7

Moving on and Letting Go

L ife is too short for holding grudges. A single grudge against someone can and will consume your life like wildfire. Now if the object of such grudges happens to be the one you're in a relationship with, then your life will be like a bottomless, dark well. Allow me to be blunt when I say that life can be quite hellish simply due to holding on to grudges. It will be filled with quarrel, chaos, and confusion, unless you make a conscious effort to find the light.

"Better to light one small candle than to curse the darkness."
—Chinese proverb

Of course, any relationship is never without problems. Fights, arguments, and discussions will naturally be there. The question lies in how you handle them. Will you hold on to your anger and let it consume your mental and emotional well-being? Or will you make an effort to let it go and forgive? It's your call entirely. Of course, my unsolicited advice would be the latter. It's so much lighter on the heart and mind. There's really no need to stress over the little things. Just let it all go, and you'll certainly be so much happier and at peace with yourself, your partner, and everyone around you.

Understanding Anger

Now before you can actually learn how to truly forgive, you must first have a deeper understanding of anger. According to ancient Vedic scriptures, "The Blessed Lord said: It is lust only, Arjuna, which is born of contact with the material modes of passion and later transformed into wrath, and which is the all-devouring, sinful enemy of this world" (Bhagavad Gita, Song of God, chapter 3, text 37).

So in this verse it is stated that wrath, or anger, is an all-devouring sin. It simply consumes your very being, causing you to lose all composure and self-control. When you're angry, you end up saying hurtful words. In the heat of the moment, you might even end up inflicting physical pain on the one you supposedly love.

In the wisdom-filled and very enlightening Vedic philosophy, the root cause of anger is the mode of passion. Allow me to share a little of what I've learned from these ancient gems of wisdom.

Different kinds of people are said to work under three modes of material nature: ignorance, passion, and goodness. People under the mode of ignorance are those that live in laziness, indifference, and apathy. Those in the mode of passion are bound by greed and lust. Those in the mode of goodness display wisdom and altruism.

In the mode of passion, you are compelled to do things you never intended to do. This is due to lust. Now, lust is a term not limited to the sexual aspect. It covers covetousness or the self-serving desire to fulfill one's own greed. In a relationship, this translates to serving your own self-interest instead of the common interests as a couple. It's when you think of no one else but yourself and never about your partner. This is considered lust, which is in the mode of passion. Sooner or later, this selfishness will take a toll on your relationship. There will be anger and shouting and tears. But all of this can be prevented by being less selfish and being more selfless. This selflessness is made possible by real love and respect, which are much easier to attain when you are in the mode of goodness.

Couples in the mode of goodness are more likely to have a lasting and peaceful relationship, while couples in the mode of passion usually have a more volatile, unstable relationship. When you are in the mode of goodness, you are more tranquil, calm, not easily angered, understanding, and forgiving. Such qualities are crucial in a relationship. A verse from the Bible further expounds: "My beloved brothers, understand this: Everyone should be quick to listen, slow to speak, and slow to anger" (James 1:19).

So how can you elevate a relationship in the mode of passion to the mode of goodness? By making a conscious effort to shift the center of your lives from yourselves toward a higher purpose. Instead of seeing your partner as someone who exists simply to serve you, seek spiritual enlightenment from successful couples who work together for a common goal.

Tusta Krishna das, an internationally known teacher of Bhakti yoga and holder of a master's degree in Gaudiya Vaishnava philosophy through the Special Majors program at Sonoma State University, gives the following tips on married life:

1. Show respect.
2. Be tolerant.
3. Be supportive.
4. Be understanding.
5. Strive for perfection yourself, but don't expect it from your partner.
6. Be encouraging.
7. Be slow to judge.

8. Apologize when you are wrong, even if the other is more wrong.
9. Be forgiving.
10. Accept responsibility for your own misery.

Whatever religious or spiritual path you are inclined to follow, whether sprouting from European or Asian influences, these tips from Tusta Krishna das are quite generic. It is basically a tried and tested path that covers all you need to know and must do to put out the all-consuming flames of lust and anger, and thus benefit from a successful relationship.

Accepting That We Are Not Perfect

You are not perfect. I am not perfect. No one is, no one has been, and no one ever will be, considering all respective aspects of a person.

When understanding and acknowledging this, the ability to forgive becomes a whole lot easier. If you set unrealistically high standards and ideals for your partner, you will be frustrated because he will undoubtedly fail in one aspect or another, at one point in time or another, because he is not perfect.

Now, try turning the situation around. Put yourself in his shoes. How would you feel if your partner imposed that you be perfect in all ways? It's a lot of pressure, right? We must learn to admit to ourselves that we are not perfect. If you admit that you do indeed have imperfections, then it will be much easier to forgive others for their imperfections.

"To err is human; to forgive, divine."
—Alexander Pope

Forgiving and Being Forgiven

I know; it's easier said than done. No, you don't have to force yourself to forgive someone when you're not really ready to. That would be superficial, and the anger would still be there in the core of your heart. What you can do is allow time to help in the healing process. Forgiveness can't be achieved overnight, especially when the wrongdoing is pretty hefty. Here's what you should do.

Remove yourself from that toxic situation. Also, avoid redundant arguments relating back to the unfortunate incident. Now, this is basically a common issue in most relationships. Like a broken record, you remind each other of your previous mistakes over and over again. Just when you think a certain issue in the past has finally found closure, it somehow finds its way to pop out in the heat of an argument, rendering old scars to open wounds yet again.

Aside from time, give it some space. Let the embers die down and avoid potential sparks. A considerable amount of breathing room is required for healing, introspection, and finally forgiveness. The time, space, and distance factors play a crucial role in the whole process. While you're in that certain heated situation, your anger will cover up your otherwise clear vision. Only after will you realize how badly you may have behaved or how hurtful your words may have been. And unfortunately, most of the time, it may be too late, and the damage done is irreparable.

Anger burns bridges, but forgiveness helps rebuild them. Of course, my advice would be to avoid confrontations when one of you is in a fit of anger. It's unwise to argue with an angry person. You can prevent a tiny spark from burning into an uncontrollable blaze by pouring water on it. Adding fuel to the fire is suicide.

For instance, if your man happens to have a volatile temper, don't anger him further. Be wise and humble enough to calm him down when necessary. You can open up to him and have a peaceful heart-to-heart talk once you see fit but not while he's in an angry state. In other words, if you truly love him, you will make an effort to find ways to go around his imperfections without creating gaps or misunderstandings. As his partner in life, you should be sensitive enough not to rub him the wrong way.

The mood of your relationship lies in your very hands. If you are tolerant, respectful, and forgiving to your man, then he will reciprocate. On the other hand, if you disrespect, ire, and nag at him, then the mood will be dark and murky. In some cultures, there is a saying that the father is the pillar of the home while the mother is the light of the home. Both have crucial functions in the family.

You, the woman, hold the light. Depending on how well you handle this responsibility, sometimes it can be very bright, and sometimes it can be dim and dreary (which is not a surprise since no one is perfect). Nonetheless, do try to avoid putting out the light altogether. A dark home devoid of love and laughter is no home at all. No matter how strong the pillars, if the home is devoid of light and warmth, no one would want to live there.

Let It Go—The Past Is in the Past

It's the best advice I can give to couples: let it go, let it go; the past is in the past.

There's really no point in holding on to grudges. Just let them go. The past is past. There's no benefit in reliving bitter memories over and over again. It will hamper the sensitive process of healing, forgiving, and moving on.

Don't let anger get the better of you. When it comes creeping in, find a healthy outlet for your emotions. Don't bottle them up. The following tips may help immensely.

Learn the art of relaxation and breathing techniques to redirect fits of anger.

Resort to prayer and meditation. If you have inner peace, peace with others comes naturally. And with this peace come forgiveness, tolerance, patience, and love.

Chapter 8

Woman's Duties to Her Man

Centuries ago, women suffered from so much oppression. They were not allowed to vote or have equal job opportunities as men. Thankfully, such oppressive boundaries have been lifted. This freedom from discrimination is encouraged in the Bible.

"There is neither Jew nor Greek, there is neither slave nor free, there is no male and female, for you are all one in Christ Jesus."
—Galatians 3:28

On the other hand, too much of anything is unhealthy. With great power comes great responsibility. Sadly, the so-called modern and liberated women of today irresponsibly put their bodies on display for the sake of "freedom of expression."

Real female empowerment is great, but not this so-called "empowerment" that simply leaves women using their newfound liberty to the extreme. Equal rights socially and legally and equal treatment in the workplace should be, of course and without debate, mandatory.

What is unacceptable and confusing in many places is when such feminists proudly expose their beach bodies in bikinis or skimpy outfits and are objectified by men or even by other women. It's natural and just to want dignity and not have to dress and behave a certain way in order to manage the behavior of others in order to be treated respectably. Another biblical verse comes to mind.

> "Do not let your adorning be external—the braiding of
> hair and the putting on of gold jewelry, or the clothing
> you wear—but let your adorning be the hidden person
> of the heart with the imperishable beauty of a gentle and
> quiet spirit, which in God's sight is very precious."
> —1 Peter 3:3–4

In this day and age, a growing number of women have become too liberated for their own good, not only in their dress code but more importantly in their behavior. Sexual promiscuity is now socially acceptable, and premarital or extramarital affairs have become "natural." Unplanned pregnancies lead to either abortion or unwanted babies left in orphanages or without a father or mother. It can be truly heart-wrenching to think that our daughters will have to grow up and be exposed to such a backward culture.

On a deeper aspect, being a submissive woman now also carries a twisted and false definition. Thus, when the subject of wifely duties comes up, no one is really interested. Rarely do we find articles in magazines or blogs about how to be a good wife or a good partner. Most often, it's all about how to spot if you're being cheated on, or how to tell if he's lying to you, or some other negative topic that simply leaves you insecure and paranoid about your relationship.

In other words, it's all about you and how to get the most out of a relationship, never about how to give more in that relationship. Also, the focus is mostly taking rather than giving, inward more than outward, self-centered instead of selfless. There are hundreds of posts on social media promoting such narcissistic views that pass as "women empowerment." No wonder divorce rates are continuing to skyrocket!

There are also dozens of write-ups on how to lose belly fat and have an awesome bikini body, how to have great hair and skin and whatnot. Yet there are none on how to be a respectable woman or a good wife. Everything is merely skin-deep.

Truly, physical beauty will diminish with disease and age, but beauty of character will not. In a truly happy home, attitude and behavior carry more weight than looks. In other words, how you treat your man is more important than how you look. Of course, there's nothing wrong with wanting to look good for him, but believe me when I say that most men care more about personality than looks.

Duties, Duties, Duties …

Although this subject is virtually taboo in the modern feministic world, allow me to boldly share what a woman should do for her man, according to ancient scriptures.

Be submissive. This is one of the main factors in a healthy relationship. This is so important that chapter 6 focuses on this subject.

"Wives, submit to your husbands, as is fitting in the Lord.
Husbands, love your wives and do not be harsh with them."
—Colossians 3:18–19

Let me reiterate, submission should be out of love and not out of fear. The art of being submissive requires a good deal of patience, tolerance, and humility. Besides, being submissive is made a lot easier if the man is an equally nice and respectful person.

Being submissive is a crucial attitude in fulfilling the various duties women face on a daily basis. I do hope the following verse serves as an enlightenment and inspiration to women.

"She is clothed with strength and dignity; she can laugh at the days to come. She speaks with wisdom, and faithful instruction is on her tongue. She watches over the affairs of her household and does not eat the bread of idleness. Her children arise and call her blessed; her husband also, and he praises her: 'Many women do noble things, but you surpass them all.' Charm is deceptive, and beauty is fleeting; but a woman who fears the Lord is to be praised."
—Proverbs 31:26–30

If you're a housewife, do household duties responsibly and lovingly, without anger. I know this is not as simple as it sounds. Being a housewife is never being "just" a housewife. There's nothing easy about maintaining a household and keeping chaos at bay, which can be extremely difficult and close to impossible when you have very young children. Nonetheless, what must be done must be done.

You will experience being a bitter or unappreciated housewife at one point or another. That's perfectly natural. You're not alone in this type of feeling. Most at-home mothers go through this. Just make sure not to wallow. Always look from a wider and deeper perspective. Sure, you may have given up your career in order to have children and take care of them the best way you can, but whatever you may have sacrificed is nothing compared to seeing your kids grow up happy and healthy.

Being a housewife and mother is like having several full-time jobs with no pay. You will have to do the laundry, the ironing, the cooking, and whatnot. And all of these should be done out of love and with the emotional support and respect of a healthy relationship. Accept with humility that your current situation, if you're not working, is that your husband happens to be the one who earns the money, and you are the one in charge of maintaining the household. It's a partnership based on respect and love.

You may be tired, but so is he. Set a lighter mood by making sure that dinner is set when he comes home from work. Strike a light conversation and ask him how his day was at work. You may also start with any good news from school, your day, or wherever. Save any bad or unpleasing news for later. Allow him to unwind first and enjoy a proper dinner instead of bombarding him with all the problems you might be having in the house or with the children's day at school. If dinner is running a little late, be creative and think of ways to help him relax while he waits. Try running a warm bath for him or play relaxing music or whatever it might be that soothes him.

Remember, this is the same man you exchanged vows with. He may be a little older, perhaps grumpier and more tired, and so are you. The responsibilities both of you have are immense, so it truly helps to remind yourselves to be more understanding of each other's flaws or shortcomings.

It helps to unwind and relax separately as individuals and together as a couple. Some massage, perhaps a cup of relaxing tea, a friendly conversation on the porch or in a calm and relaxing place, a little moonlit stroll, or separately reading your favorite books before bedtime are some time-tested tips from successful couples.

Treat him as your friend and not as someone you want to nag, dominate, and control. Never nag your husband. Doing so is like hitting your relationship with a wrecking ball. Afterward, you will be left picking up the broken pieces and hurt yourself in the process.

"In the same way, their wives are to be women worthy of respect, not malicious talkers but temperate and trustworthy in everything."
—Timothy 3:11

In the morning, the wife should wake up early to prepare her husband's clothes as well as put a nice breakfast on the table. Doing these very basic things day in and day out may not seem like much to you sometimes, yet they are everything to your family.

Imagine what mornings would be like if you weren't around. Your poor husband and children would be in sheer chaos! Now, imagine if *they* were not around every morning. Yes, you might sleep in until noon and have no worries about the endless menial duties, but would you really choose this over your loved ones?

Sometimes it helps to step back a bit and try looking from a different perspective. In this way, you become more appreciative of the people in your life and you can better fulfill your duties with more love and care.

In a real loving relationship, it doesn't really matter if you're the one left with the menial tasks. Out of love, you wish to please him in whatever way you can. Now, in modern-day scenarios when you happen to be the breadwinner and he is the house-husband, your main duty to him is to make him feel loved and appreciated, just as you would want to be treated yourself.

He may be the one who's left with all the menial tasks and babysitting, yet he remains your lifelong partner whom you should respect and love nonetheless. He is humble, considerate, and understanding enough to accept the other end of the line without ego. A man like that is rare and should be cause for appreciation and celebration. Love and respect him even more.

"However, let each one of you love his wife as himself,
and let the wife see that she respects her husband."
—Ephesians 5:33

Trying to Change Your Man?

It won't happen! Most men are unbending when you try to change them when it comes down to their emotions. Yes, ladies, we men get emotional too. However, when a man meets the right woman, he will be more than willing to change certain behavior or traits that he has, given he's supported in his efforts.

When a man meets the right woman, he might be very willing to open up his emotions to his woman. Men generally do not divulge their emotions much more than things that are bothering them. But when a man exhibits strong emotions for a woman, he is much more willing to open up and communicate what he is feeling deep inside.

While some men are not good at talking about what they are feeling, they might be better able to open up when they don't feel pressured to do so. Most men do not talk about their feelings because they do not want to bother or upset you with their troubles. But allow a man to talk about how his day was or anything that is bugging him by casually asking him about it. If a man is pressured to pour his heart out, you might not get what you want out of him.

Another mistake some women make when looking for Mr. Right is thinking that he will truly live up to his name or reputation of being romantic and all. And that he will precisely know what makes you happy. You have to let him know what you want out of your relationship, and you should ask for it.

It is not sensible to conclude that your partner will know exactly what you want. There are even bigger possibilities that both of you have contrasting ways of showing love and affection. To get what you want out of your man, you need to ask for what you want or need and then give him positive reinforcement when he gets or does things that please you.

Aside from that, it's not always on your man to be romantic; believe it or not, some of us men like to be romanced too. This will keep the romance between you alive. You can pick him up after work or treat him for a romantic dinner sometime.

Being Reserved Only for Your Man

Being reserved for your man, not only physically but emotionally, can be the noblest thing a woman can do. This is not only for herself but for when the right man comes along. When a woman values herself, she values every aspect in her life.

In today's world where everyone is looking for instant gratification, a woman who wholly reserves herself for the right man is very hard to find. Such a woman who does not look into the worldly things and has control over herself, physically, emotionally, and mentally is a great gift from God.

Moreover, if you look at things from a different perspective, sex can poison the best relationships. When sex becomes the focus of a relationship, you cease to get to know each other at different levels. Rather than grow beside or with one another, you actually start to drift apart. This happens in all aspects of your relationship, be it emotionally, physically, mentally, or spiritually.

When physical longing becomes the center of a relationship, it disengages other parts of the relationship. As a consequence, the relationship starts to wander off in a different direction. I've witnessed so many couples who would have had a great relationship but wandered into physical longing and ended up breaking each other apart. I too have experienced this.

Furthermore, when a woman easily gives herself up to a man, there is a greater tendency for a man to lose respect for that woman, even if he doesn't want to. A woman, on the other hand, might lose trust in her man even though she doesn't intend to. This is engraved in the perception of a lot of people. There are couples who run into marital problems because they previously were engaged in premarital sex. They jump into a relationship without respect for each other and with absence of trust, which is an unconditional prerequisite for a healthy affair.

Some now have the mind-set of, *If he or she cheated on him or her with me, then they'll cheat on me.* There goes the trust from the start.

In addition, sex to some may mean an approval of the relationship, but it shouldn't be the most significant aspect of it. It should be considered the cherry on top when all other aspects of the relationship are working perfectly together. Sex can be satisfying only if everything in the relationship is going well.

Be Willing to Give

Just being there for your man to support him in everything that he does is more than enough to make your man feel that he is special. Sometimes, even when you are in a loving relationship, it can be hard to give the time and energy needed to show your man how much he truly means to you. And there may be moments when you feel like you have neglected your man, so you need to make it up to him. For the most part, a man does not require too much brouhaha, just your special attention to make him feel that he is loved and appreciated.

A woman must also be willing to give in order to contribute to the relationship. Most of the time, it is expected of the man make the effort, but men appreciate it when the woman exerts a little effort for him as well.

Most of the time, a man will fall for a woman who shows romantic gestures to him. A romantic little kiss when he is watching television leaves him mellow and wanting to cuddle his woman. This lets a man know that the woman truly cares about him. Even a simple gesture like cooking his favorite meal shows this. There has always been truth to the old saying, the way to a man's heart is through his stomach. A man will be more than appreciative of the time and effort a woman puts in to keep him satisfied.

Nonetheless, being affectionate to your man is one of the simplest things you can do to show that you care for your man. We sometime are so engrossed in our everyday lives we forget the significance of the human touch. Getting a little emotional and touching your man once in a while can rekindle the spark between both of you. A simple kiss before he goes to work or a hug when he least expects it leaves your man wanting you more.

More than anything else, being there when your man needs you can be the most important thing you can do to make your man feel cared for. Talking to your man and being a good listener when he talks is also a significant part of a secure, strong, and healthy relationship.

Chapter 9

Material Love versus Spiritual Love

Without knowledge of spiritual love, all the so-called love you may have experienced or are experiencing now is actually based on just the material or superficial aspect. It is not real love in the truest sense of the word. There are many faces of "love" in this world, and unfortunate as it can be, these are what have been passing as love for centuries already.

Infatuation

Nothing but a passing sentiment, the passionate intensity of infatuation is short-lived. You only think you're in love with someone, but you're actually not. It's comparable to puppy love. It's a mere phase that comes and goes quite quickly. It's like obsessing over something, but once you get that something, you find that it doesn't really satisfy you. Another analogy is like chewing gum and spitting it out once the sweetness is gone. You're simply tired and fed up with it. A relationship rooting from infatuation does not last. This is because we see other people as mere objects of enjoyment and not as real people. This is also based on lust.

Lust

This is what generally passes as love. So how does it differ from actual love? Lust is all about taking; love is more about giving. In a relationship of lust, we are always thinking about what we can get out of that other person instead of what we can give. It's self-centered, self-absorbed, and selfish. You do things for someone and please them but all the while having the ulterior motive of gaining some benefit in return. In other words, you simply wish to please yourself in the long run. There's no actual care for the other person. You're simply using him for some self-serving hidden agenda.

Material Love

This is better than lust, of course. However, it does have its limits. We may love somebody and care about their well-being but only to a certain extent. It's bound by the boundaries of the material aspect. You love someone because he is physically handsome or good-looking. When he loses an arm or a leg or burns his face in a fire, you start "falling out of love."

This proves that, in the very beginning, your love was based on the superficial, material aspect. You fell in love with his body and not him, the person dwelling inside that external body. This is material love. It's all physical really. If you don't see your husband or boyfriend for months or years (perhaps he's working abroad or something), you also begin "falling out of love" and begin looking for a new person who is physically present. Time, space, and distance wear off this so-called love. Real love, on the other hand, is the opposite. It is not bound by time, space, and distance ... and not even by material considerations.

Real Love

Real love is spiritual in nature. The Vedic philosophy teaches that we are not the material body we see in the mirror. We are the spiritual beings temporarily residing in these material bodies. Our love and respect for each other should not be shallowly based on the physical aspect or any other material consideration.

When you truly love someone, you will continue loving that person even if he is not as young and attractive as he used to be. You will still love him even if his hair turns gray, his skin wrinkles, and his body is not as fit and as strong as it was when you first met him. You will love him through thick and thin, in sickness and in health, till death do you part. This is called unconditional love.

Real love means loving the person inside the body and not just his external shell. You love him for who he really is—a spiritual being who is a child of God. Once you understand that we are all children of one God, you will truly learn to love other people. You will treat them with respect and continue loving them no matter what changes happen to their body.

While lust and material "love" are self-seeking, love is selfless.

> "Love is patient, love is kind. It does not envy, it does not
> boast, it is not proud. It is not rude, it is not self-seeking,
> is not easily angered, it keeps no account of wrongs."
> —1 Corinthians 4–5

What Women Want in a Man

Not to generalize all people, but *most* want a partner who is good-looking, well to do, doting, and romantic. The order of importance of these traits may vary from one person to another, but these are often the cornerstones of what people tend to look for in a companion. Of course, I can't speak for others, especially women; I can't even speak for just one woman. But based on my personal observations, from the outside looking in, these are important preferences people tend to have for potential mates.

Good-looking. Naturally, we are attracted to beauty. Women want their homes and gardens to be pleasant. When they go window-shopping, they sometimes end up impulsively buying pretty little things they don't really need. Of course, this isn't true for all women, and it can even apply to some men.

My point is that it is only human nature to be attracted to beauty and to be attracted to beautiful people. Men naturally want someone pretty, and women want someone handsome. There's nothing wrong with this. The physical aspect is basically what has initially attracted us to our partners. But we must try to go beyond the physical and deepen our relationship.

Men should learn to love their wives in all ways, and women must learn to love their husbands faithfully and unconditionally despite their physical imperfections, which will in due time increase with age. You must learn to love the person that he truly is inside and not just how he appears.

Well-to-do and doting. Of course, not all women desire a rich husband, but there are a good many of them who do. You can see this in young and beautiful gold-diggers who marry the old and rich for some other ulterior motive other than love. These women enjoy a lavish display of affection from their doting husbands. Of course, we are not in the position to judge a woman by her choice of man. After all, we can't really tell if it's out of love or not. It's none of our business really.

But this is just to cite an example relevant to the topic of real versus material love. The point is that you can tell if a relationship is really based on love or not when the husband becomes bankrupt and penniless. If the wife truly loves her husband, she will stick by him no matter what. If she flees, then the marriage was conditional. From the very beginning, she was more interested in the person's wealth and not in the person himself.

Of course, with all due respect to all women reading this, I am not typecasting women in general. My goal is to present what some women tend to want in a man, as a precursor to the next topic, which is what women should want in a man.

What Women Should Want in a Man

It's increasingly normal for young girls to dream of finding their rich and handsome prince who will love them and obey their each and every whim. However, such dreams seldom come true. You cannot really come across a perfect person because no one is perfect in the truest sense of the word.

For instance, a man can be very handsome yet poor as a pauper. Or he can be very rich but not too easy on the eyes. Or he can be both rich and handsome but not very true and loyal. In other words, finding the perfectly ideal man is close to impossible.

There is no need to set unreasonably high standards and ideals when you yourself are not perfect. Instead of chasing a mirage, accept the reality of the situation. Physical looks slowly but surely depreciate with age, and money comes and goes. The women who marry for looks or money alone usually end up with their marriage in shambles, so why follow suit? It's like following a blind person who has fallen into a ditch.

So what should you look for in a man? Here are some qualities of men that are worth your while.

Good Character

What use is his handsome face or his million dollars if he's rotten on the inside? Money may be the solution to some things but not to everything. Surely, it can save you from a lot of headache and anxiety. You can be spared from the draining task of regularly looking for money to pay the rent and the bills and to put food on the table. It may satisfy your basic physical well-being but not necessarily your emotional well-being. He may lavishly clothe you with designer dresses and diamonds, but he may not treat you as nicely.

In the long run, his face will wrinkle, and his strong muscles will atrophy with age. Better to have an average-looking man with a hole in his pocket but a big heart than to have a devilishly good-looking one with a heavy pocket but poor character.

Now if you happen to be blessed with a husband that is nice-looking, financially decent, and with great character, then lucky you! Appreciate and be thankful for him. As I've said before, it truly helps to every once in a while take a step back and look at things from a different perspective. Otherwise, you might not know what you're missing.

Honest, Responsible, and Hardworking

It is only natural to consider the practical financial aspect when entering marriage. Of course, if you intend to start a family, you naturally think about money. A husband should be responsible and hardworking for his family. It's always better to have just enough money to be able to make ends meet honestly and responsibly than having excessive amounts of money obtained through unethical or unscrupulous means.

Respectful

Although chivalry in men has long been suffering a slow and agonizing death, fortunately it has not totally been extinguished. A man who is respectful in his words, thoughts, and actions is admirable. Love and respect are inseparable. You are very lucky indeed if you ever find a true gentleman who will love and respect you instead of control and dominate you.

Intelligent

In this context, I am not referring to being brilliantly brainy but to being insightful and introspective. A truly intelligent man is one who is intuitive enough to inquire into the higher and deeper purpose of life and existence. He is humble enough to accept his shortcomings as a man and thus seek help from a higher being.

In other words, he believes in the existence of God in some way or another and tries to live morally. He uses his intelligence for further spiritual enlightenment instead of wasting time and energy on the temporary, shallow, and fleeting things in this world. Absorbed in meditation and prayer, such a husband is calm in temper, more respectful, more understanding, and more loving.

A godless husband, on the other hand, is most likely prone to immorality, infidelity, and dishonesty. This is because he does not accept that there is a higher being above him and thus does not feel accountable to anyone at all. He is his own god and will do as he pleases, all morality aside.

The Manipulative Nature of a Woman

In the first chapter, we talked about the nature of women. In this chapter, we will further tackle the third type of woman, the fox, which can be very manipulative in nature.

Some women can be manipulative, and that's a hard fact. Even women themselves acknowledge this truth about some of their fellow women. Of course, the tendency to manipulate and control others is an intrinsic part of human nature in both men and women. However, this manipulative nature can be quite alarming when displayed in women.

For one, it is more difficult to detect. The deceptive genius can hide perfectly behind an angelic and innocent façade. When such cunning women get to work, they usually succeed in getting whatever they want. And this can be very scary. Such women have destroyed lives. Almost without any conscience, they continue to wreak havoc in otherwise happy relationships and healthy businesses.

So what is behind this manipulative nature in women? The driving force behind it is lust, greed, and selfishness—abominable qualities that cause pain and suffering to everyone around them and ultimately to themselves. All the pain they cause will come back to them in due time. According to the Vedic philosophy, for every action there is a reaction. This is the law of karma. The Bible also says: "As you sow, so shall you reap." So no good ever comes out of being manipulative, greedy, and selfish.

However, women who have a history or a tendency of being manipulative always have a chance to change. This manipulative nature can be curbed by spiritual enlightenment and love. In real love, there is no room for lust, greed, and self-centeredness. In love, you become vulnerable and let your guard down to invite someone into your heart.

The urge to manipulate and dominate becomes less and less because you want to respect the freedom of the one you love. Truly, love conquers all.

"Love does not dishonor others, it is not self-seeking, it is not easily angered, it keeps no record of wrongs. Love does not delight in evil but rejoices with the truth."
—1 Corinthians 13:5–6

Chapter 10

Become a Bee, Not a Fly

I may not be a woman, but I am certainly not oblivious of the hardships of being one. I do have a fairly accurate idea or two based on personal interactions with the many important women in my life, as well as from careful observations of the ever-changing roles of women in modern society. My heart goes out to all mothers, daughters, sisters, girlfriends, and wives who have to endure all the physical, mental, and emotional troubles that continue to afflict and bombard them ferociously on a daily basis, on both the personal and social levels.

Somehow understanding such difficulties associated with womanhood, I wish to leave a friendly tip from one human being to another. In my heart of hearts, I truly wish that this will be accepted and understood in a positive light: *become a bee and not a fly.*

The Loathsome Fly

A fly thrives and revels in repulsive living conditions. From the maggot stage to adulthood, it practically feeds on decaying matter. Attracted to all things dirty and rotten, it even takes delight in fecal matter. Aside from happily feasting on the unthinkable, it also haphazardly spreads deadly diseases, infecting many unsuspecting and otherwise healthy families.

Unfortunately, there are people who are comparable to the loathsome fly. An obvious example is shallow and useless celebrity news that is made simply for the purpose of bashing famous people by intruding on their private lives. The people behind this are like flies that feast on unhealthy trivial issues and gossip. They misuse the power of the media and simply spread hate and controversy.

Sadly, young minds become accustomed to reading and watching such a waste of time. On a deeper level, they inadvertently expose themselves to subliminal messages that bring about negative and destructive views, attitudes, and behaviors. These young people then subconsciously learn to adapt and apply horrendous conduct on the personal level, where they also become faultfinders, gossipers, and rumormongers, and they enjoy taking part in such a degraded way of thinking.

The new generation is taught to judge a person by the way she looks, what brand she wears, how she wears her hair and makeup, and some other silly and superficial thing. Body shaming and cyber bullying have become so rampant that even people as young as nine or ten years old have learned to pick up on such nasty habits. Relationships have thus become shallow, superficial, and disposable, all because we no longer see each others as real people but as objects of enjoyment.

Unfortunate as it can be, this is true. We judge other people by what they look like on the outside. But that external shell will sooner or later become riddled with disease or old age.

Ultimately, this external shell that once was so attractive will decompose and rot. If we then base our relationships on the physical, superficial aspect, in the long run we will simply be like ignorant flies that feast on decaying matter.

Be Like a Bee

The bee is an admirable creature. While flies are attracted to feces and all things disgusting, bees are attracted only to the sweet nectar from flowers. They live solely on this nectar, toiling day in and day out to serve their queen and produce honey for their young. Bees are very organized and loyal. One species, the honeybee, will even give up its own life for the sake and safety of its queen and the entire hive, instantly dying after stinging. It is a selfless creature that puts his hive before himself.

A far cry from the loathsome fly that simply spreads disease, the regal and noble bee also pollinates the flowers from which they collect nectar. In other words, how they live benefits everyone around them, including plants, animals, and humans, and not just themselves. We should be more like bees and not like flies.

When it comes to relationships, we can learn so much from bees. They are clean, organized, loyal, and hardworking for the entire family. They are never alone because they are good team workers. You should be as industrious as the bee and work hard for the benefit of your loved ones, leaving little room for idleness.

> "She watches carefully all that goes on throughout her
> household and does not eat the bread of idleness."
> —Proverbs 21:27

> "Idle hands are the devil's workshop; idle lips are his mouthpiece."
> —Proverbs 16:27

We should not be like flies that revel in chaos, disorder, self-interest, and filth; we should be more like bees and revel in order, organization, purpose, health, selflessness, loyalty, and general interest.

Like bees, we should be attracted to sweet nectar and not to decomposing matter. We must learn to see and appreciate a person's real inner beauty and sweetness and not see him simply on the physical platform, which will sooner or later decompose.

In a different context, you should be like a bee and focus on your husband's strengths and good qualities, and not be like a fly that focuses on his faults and shortcomings instead. Allow me to refresh your memory on Tusta Krishna das's tip number 5 from chapter 7: strive for perfection yourself but never expect it from your spouse.

Chapter 11

Be the Woman God Wants You to Be

Being a modern woman doesn't necessitate being a godless one. In addition, being a godly person doesn't necessarily mean having to shun all forms of modernity or technology, as some of these can be quite practical and useful. Your lifestyle can be modern in many ways yet morally and spiritually sound as well. You must only be extra careful, selective, discerning, and thoughtful about how you utilize such modern tools. After all, too much of anything is never healthy.

The smartphone, for instance, is indeed very handy. However, it is also overly used in taking selfies, which are actually a modern awakening of narcissism or physical vanity. While this gadget can be used for practical purposes, it can also be a means to exacerbate self-absorption. This also means increasingly identifying with our physical appearances and thus relating to others based on the superficial, external aspect instead of the essential person inside.

> "It is only with the heart that one can see rightly;
> what is essential is invisible to the eye."
> —Antoine de Saint-Exupery, *The Little Prince*

The Godless Woman versus the Godly Woman

Unfortunately, due to the absence of some form of moral regulation or another, many modern women today end up exposed, exploited, abused, and burned out either by the music, movie, or fashion business, which aid in the objectification of women. Such industries set unrealistically high standards of so-called beauty in women, pushing young girls to the limits and turning them into bulimics and anorexics with an insatiably poor self-image. Many girls literally starve themselves half to death or break a rib or two in waist training, all for the sake of attaining the much-coveted flat belly and trim waist. Or they resort to plastic surgery for that "perfect" figure made ideal by fashion models and celebrities. This is the message passed on to the younger generation: that you are your body and how you are treated will depend on appearances instead of character and personality.

> "Do not let your adornment be merely outward—arranging the hair, wearing gold, or putting on fine apparel—rather let it be the hidden person of the heart, with the incorruptible beauty of a gentle and quiet spirit, which is very precious in the sight of God."
> —1 Peter 3:3–4

On a deeper note, young women are taught that they are the center of their own universe and should "follow their heart," a trite slogan overly misused to actually mean: "Do whatever you want with your life. No rules. No regulations. Sky's the limit." In other words, you are your own boss, as opposed to the boss being a higher being or a holy book. As a matter of fact, the mere mention of God, religion, spirituality, or even morality is virtually taboo, uncool, and embarrassing. You are considered a "normal" girl when you wear revealing clothes, party and get drunk two or three times a week, and engage in one-night stands with total strangers on a regular basis; and you are weird when you dress conservatively, don't party and mingle, and attend worship. Everything's upside down and inside out.

All of this backward philosophy implicates the relationship aspect. Being her own boss, the godless woman dominates over her partner just for the sake of false ego. Their relationship fails because of pride and lack of submission. But basically, all problems are rooted in godlessness. Following no basic life principles regarding spirituality, or some form of morality at the least, such women practically become too liberated for their own good. They follow the bidding of their own selfish desires, without any regard for spiritual or moral values. In other words, being godless and not feeling accountable to anyone else above them, they are their own god. They follow every single selfish whim, despite potentially hurting everyone around them in the process.

They answer only to themselves and not to anyone else. Such is the twisted philosophy of what passes as modern feminism, which has become misunderstood and misrepresented as having the freedom to do everything without limit or regulation. So-called self-expression now equals wearing skimpy outfits, and being "liberated" now equals having the liberty to flirt with various men and enjoy sexual promiscuity. They divorce, remarry, divorce again, and remarry again until it becomes a habit and their hearts become calloused and hard. Having shunned control and regulation, they thus end up exploited, ultimately living a frustrated, unhappy, empty, purposeless, and meaningless life.

This is so unfortunate. You need not experience such suffering, which can be avoided or at least minimized simply by being the kind of woman God wants you to be.

"Charm is deceitful and beauty is vain,
But a woman who fears the Lord, she shall be praised."

—Proverbs 31:30

Simply by understanding and applying the basic knowledge and truth that you are not your physical body but the spiritual being within, and that others are also spiritual beings and children of the same supreme Father, you can learn to love and respect yourself, your partner, and everyone else. You can learn to relate to others soul to soul and not just on the bodily basis. By being the woman God wants you to be, you will no longer see your partner as someone to control, dominate and manipulate, but as your friend, better half, and partner in life.

"An excellent wife who can find?
For her worth is far above jewels. The heart
of her husband trusts in her,
And he will have no lack of gain.
She does him good and not evil all the days of her life."
—Proverbs 31:10–12

Chapter 12

Balancing Personal and Relationship Obligations

I have never liked the concept of obligations in a relationship, not even the use of the terms "be in debt," "demand," or "expect" when having a discussion with the one that I'm in a relationship with. When it comes to obligations in a relationship, it is never a requirement to coerce someone to do anything that he or she does not want to do.

Naturally, in most personal relationships, regardless of the nature of them, romantic or otherwise, we don't consider people owing anything to us, rightfully claiming or expecting something in return for what we give or do for them. It has to come naturally from us if we owe something to someone to reciprocate what they do.

Nonetheless, in the dynamics of human relationships, this is something that is fully understood and not talked about, something that is fully given in return. In relationships where obligations are forced and demanded, the relationship starts to sink and deteriorate. In such instances where a couple counts the number of favors one gives to the other and then expects some kind of indulgence, the relationship becomes miserable because it lessens the passion and romance.

The relationship becomes more like a balance sheet where there are liens and credits that need to be balanced off. It can be a good way to administer a business or run a household but an awful way to engage a relationship.

In one philosopher's view about obligations, there is a clear distinction between being obliged to do something and bearing the obligation to do something. In the context of relationships, a woman may feel obligated toward her partner. But she recognizes this as part of who she is and essentially becomes the meaning of what that relationship is to her. She is inclined to value the relationship, value her partner, and as such, she is instinctively obliged to act jointly in it. If a woman values sincerity and honesty, she would naturally feel the obligation to be open and faithful. If a woman values loyalty, then she would feel the obligation to be devoted.

Chapter 13

Handling Relationship Issues

All relationships have ups and downs. It is but natural to have some arguments down the road, but this does not have to be the measure of your love for each other. Frustration and anger toward a partner do not have to be detrimental to the relationship. Ultimately, it all boils down to how both of you manage your problems together.

Handling relationship issues can be hard, especially if the problem is deep-rooted. But nothing gets solved when both of you are emotionally heated. It just ends up in finger pointing, causing many grievances on both sides.

It is important to know that with every situation, there are two problems; one is your emotions, and the second is the categorical problem. In most situations, you are dealing with being upset or frustrated, and the other is the actual issue itself. Nonetheless, you have to make a choice of prioritizing the issues and dealing with them separately.

In addition, you may also want to consider having a more productive discussion rather than just being irrational about the problem. When you are incensed by your loved one, airing your resentments can be the worst thing you can do. If you are emotionally heated, it is best to calm down first before starting to talk about an impending issue.

Certainly, it is normal to vent our anger and frustration, although brooding on the problem and not showing any action will just keep you incensed. So typically, you have to deal with your emotions first and deal with your stress before getting into a discussion. It is important to know that stomping off and mumbling under your breath is an immediate way of stinging someone.

So, before getting into an argument, you might want to tell your loved one what you need to do in order to get out of a heated confrontation. A simple statement like, "I need to calm myself down," or, "Let's just talk in a few minutes," can be more helpful than uttering useless words like, "Whatever!"

Once you have control over yourself, you can deal with the situation more effectively. Remember, when having a temper, we lose our capacity for logical thinking, empathy, and productive problem solving. It is also good if there is collaborative partnering and not fighting against each other. This way, both of you become more productive and are able to resolve your issues much better.

Chapter 14

Healing over Failed Relationships

A failed relationship can send your emotions in different directions. It can either send you spiraling downward, arousing old thinking patterns and gathering pessimistic convictions about yourself, or it can be an enormous road for personal improvement. It depends on how you see a failed relationship and the approach you take from it.

Admitting that it takes a lot of effort to heal yourself and to reconcile with your mind-set, learning how to heal yourself rather than letting those difficult emotions linger is eventually more helpful for you.

The very first thing you may want to consider is letting go. Take your time to mourn the lost relationship. Let your emotions run, as this is helpful in getting over the ruined relationship. Allow yourself to cry if you have to and accept the fact that it is all over.

Eventually, giving yourself time to reflect helps you get over the failed relationship. You do not need to rush into a new relationship just to get even with your ex or because you feel like you cannot be without a man in your life. This will only make things more complicated as you make way for another possible heartbreak.

It is also important to recognize negative thoughts like bitterness, regret, and guilt, as they can be crippling emotions that hinder you from moving forward. Nonetheless, recognizing emotional triggers can prevent a stockpile of emotional issues in the long run.

Another thing to consider is discontinuing your communication with your ex. You have to stop connecting with him so you can move on with your life. It is never good to continue sending him e-mails or text messages when it is over, especially if he, just like you, is trying to move on. This can be a hard part of healing, as you have gotten used to revolving around his presence.

Getting rid of all the things that remind you of your ex can also be good for your healing. This just simply shows your readiness to move forward with your life. Although, once you have gotten over the failed relationship, you can simply become no more than friends or associates. This can be good for both of you, running into the same circle of friends that both of you may already have.

Healing over a failed relationship can be hard at the start, but once you let go of all the things that might have been, your world will be more bright and colorful. And once you have done so, you can catch up with your friends and family. Getting into another relationship can take time, but when you do, you will be wiser than before.

Chapter 15

Four Key Characteristics to Strengthen Relationships

B eing in a relationship can be exhilarating, but it can also be exhausting. It can even drive you to the brink of insanity sometimes, especially during the first few years of adjustment as a new couple. This is perhaps one of the most critical period in a couple's life. You get irked by each other's little habits that you never noticed before. Your partner complains about how long you take when using the bathroom, and you get annoyed when he constantly leaves the toilet seat up. The list is virtually endless, from the most minute and trivial details up to more serious ones such as suspicions of infidelity.

Marriage on the Rocks

The girlfriend-boyfriend stage is one thing; the married stage is a whole new and unknown world. It's when you start living together in the same house that you get to actually know the unexplored side of your better half. It's only then when you can find out if he's a highly organized person or a total slob. Married life is when all the strengths and weaknesses of your spouse will be unraveled, sometimes subtly and sometimes bluntly without warning. There will be many times when you will feel like you are treading totally unfamiliar, unchartered waters, and things can get pretty dark, scary, awkward, and out of hand.

Separation Is Never the Answer, Real Love Is

If you start sensing a potentially rocky downfall in your relationship, separation should not be seen as the instant solution. Walking out on your relationship is a form of escape from facing the bitter truth that the problem actually lies within each of you. The problem lies within you, and this very same problem will still be there even when you go your separate ways. If you enter into a relationship again, the probability of it ending up with the same fate as your first one is high, because the problem remains unaddressed and unresolved. You may be relating to a different person now, yet the problems you will be facing may inherently be the same.

You might have noticed this very same issue in celebrity relationships, which seldom last. They fall in love and get married, and then a couple of years or even months down the road, they divorce. A few months later or even almost immediately, they start seeing other people, get married, and then get divorced again. It's an endless cycle, this search for the perfect partner. You may think that finally you have come across an oasis, but once you're there, you discover that you have been chasing a mirage all along. And so you move on and start chasing another mirage. Not only is this exhausting, it is also quite ridiculous.

Stop chasing mirages. Get out of the desert. In other words, stop looking for the perfect man. Look within you instead. Admit and accept that the problem may in fact lie within you or within both of you. This is the first step to strengthening your relationship: acknowledging that he is not perfect and you are not perfect, thus being able to accurately identify certain points that need tweaking. Otherwise, all future relationships will suffer the same fate.

Learning and applying the following values can hopefully help you save and strengthen your relationship.

Humility

Once you learn the art of being humble, you increase your chances of saving your relationship. People have too much pride, and it is what usually breaks up relationships. Due to pride, no one is humble enough to say sorry or ask for forgiveness. Due to pride, no one knows how to really listen anymore.

For instance, when you have a verbal fight with your man, your pride and his pride clash. You talk while he talks. Neither one of you is humble enough to respectfully stop and listen to what the other person is trying to say. You one-sidedly want to give him a piece of your mind, and he tries to do the same with you. And thus, the argument is left unresolved simply because of too much pride in both parties. Neither one is humble enough to give way and respectfully listen to the other person's side.

Or sometimes it may appear that you are listening but are actually not. It might be that you are simply plotting and thinking of a rebuttal against whatever he might be saying. And he may do the same thing to you as well. Although both of you may appear to be listening, in reality, you might not be. Most often, both of you are too proud to actually listen and accept defeat. And then upon noticing that he's not listening, you start raising your voice, and he reciprocates. Sooner or later, you will be yelling at each other, as if the volume is the problem and the reason why you can't hear each other. Yet the main problem lies not in the volume of your voice but in your proud hearts, and you refuse to hold your horses and actually listen.

Another example is when you are engaged in a cold war with your partner. Based on my experience, it is quite normal for women to give their men the cold shoulder or the silent treatment when offended. This is usually the case with sensitive women who are not at all naggers but quite the opposite. They simply clam up and wage a silent war by refusing to engage in a conversation with their partners—not even small talk!

And the cold and silent war can go on and on and on for weeks, until the trivial tiff gradually but significantly creates a gap, which cannot be bridged unless one of you is humble enough to break the ice and apologize. Pride holds you back from apologizing for the sake of putting an end to this dragging and emotionally exhausting mind game.

Tip number 8 in chapter 7 thus comes into mind: *apologize when you are wrong, even if the other is more wrong.* If your man is a little sensitive and has enough common sense, he will appreciate your humble move and will not want to add insult to injury by repeating his mistake. Your maturity will sober him up a bit, and he will behave more maturely himself the next time around.

Tolerance

If this word sounds alien to you, then now is the time to add it to your vocabulary and start applying it to real life. Tolerance basically means the ability to tolerate or put up with the things that you don't really like or approve of. However, note that this attitude has two faces; it can either be beneficial or destructive, depending on the particular situations you apply it to.

In a relationship, for instance, it is sound to apply tolerance to petty issues you tend to raise against your man, such as his leaving the toilet seat up, forgetting to hang his coat upon entering the house, talking while his mouth is full, or some other little habits that are annoying to you. In lighter situations like these, it is healthy for you to be tolerant of his little flaws and imperfections. After all, if you put yourself in his shoes and try looking at your own habits from his angle, you will find that you also have little issues that may be annoying *to him*. It will be healthier and more peaceful if you remain tolerant of each other's little faults and let minor issues slide.

Now, if you discern that he has real issues that truly need resolving, then you should not tolerate or condone them just for the sake of avoiding a confrontation. Tolerance should not be applied in this context. Not saying anything can actually make things worse. If, for instance, your man's habits start swaying to the verge of illegal, or something physically or mentally destructive (such as alcohol or drug abuse), then you should not, in any way, tolerate this.

Love means disregarding and overlooking your little differences, but love also means helping him see the bigger picture about his majorly destructive issues. Give him time. Show attention, care, and support. And never *ever* nag at him.

Men are deeply annoyed by naggers. The more you nag, the less we tend to listen. Believe me, it's no joke that the minute you start nagging, we make use of our invisible earplugs and simply go to our *happy place*. Or, if you're not so fortunate, there are men who will just snap and physically hurt you.

Anyway, for the sake of both parties, it is safer to avoid nagging. Instead, try a different approach. Use your creative, complex, and (sometimes) manipulative thought processes to devise a plan on how you can get your message across to your man without offending him or making him want to wear his invisible earplugs. With a little sensitivity, you can make your move during his best time of the day when he's most receptive and calm. Being more laid back and gentle in your approach also reaps more positive results. Tell him that it is because you're worried and care for him that you want to talk things through.

It is never good to force him to change; that change must come from him. As an analogy, you can only do so much to bring the horse to the water, but you cannot drink the water for the horse. Simply be supportive and understanding of the current phase he may be going through. Now, it is only after showing his willingness and determination to change that you can again start applying tolerance. Progress cannot be achieved overnight. He will, time and again, fall down, and it is during these critical times that he needs you to be extremely tolerant of his faults along the way.

Patience

Tolerance has an identical twin—patience. Although these two may be very similar indeed and one is often mistaken for the other, they still remain as two different and individual qualities. Tolerance is being able to respectfully accept and put up with differences and handle difficult situations despite such differences. Patience is the quality of being forbearing—waiting calmly and coolly without losing composure or your head.

A crude example is waiting in line for something. You're in a great hurry and are almost late for an appointment, yet here you find yourself stuck in a long queue, and you have no other choice but to wait. If you have not enough patience, you might resort to cutting in line to the annoyance of everyone around you. If you are patient enough, you can remain composed and stay in your current post, understanding that you are not the center of the universe and that those people behind and in front of you also have their own personal engagements but choose to keep their head and stay in line.

A deeper example is the art of bonsai, which should never be rushed.

In order to craft a decent bonsai, the bonsai enthusiast must have truckloads and truckloads of patience in planting, wiring, pruning, repotting, and whatnot. Otherwise, the branches will break, the desired design will not materialize, or the tree will die.

Caring for a plant is really not that different from caring for a person. Lots of tender, loving care and patience is necessary in order to successfully grow a garden. You should be sensitive to the basic needs of the plants, making sure they are met and satisfied on a regular basis. Most important of all is your patience. A seedling cannot grow a meter high overnight. If you rush it by overwatering or over-applying fertilizer, the plant will wither and die. Without patience, your relationship will also suffer the same fate.

You should be tolerant of your man's flaws and hope that he will also be tolerant enough of yours. Be patient and hopeful that your relationship can withstand the sometimes cold and harsh test of time, weather, and circumstances; be healthier and more mature; bloom and bear fruit.

God-centeredness

Any relationship will naturally have problems. That's a given. If your relationship is based on lust and self-centeredness, these problems are tripled; if your relationship is based on material or conditional love, then such problems may not be as much. Now if your relationship is on the spiritual platform of God-centeredness, your problems become halved, quartered, or even less.

A relationship based on material love is obviously a little better than one based on lust. However, they are like two sides of the same coin. They are very fleeting and temporary because both lack the essential principles of real, spiritual love.

"Love does not consist in gazing at each other, but in
looking outward together in the same direction."
—Antoine de Saint-Exupery

The quote above is so true. And that specific "same direction" is God. In reality, God is the missing link in all relationships. Some people might not welcome or accept the idea, but the argument behind it is quite sound.

By making God the center of your relationship, there is less room for jealousy, which is a one-eyed monster that slowly and silently creeps into selfish relationships. If you understand that your partner is a child of God, then you can take better care of him and learn to love and respect him unconditionally. Knowing that you don't own him and that God does, you will not strive to control or dominate him. Without God at the core, your relationship is bound to fail sooner or later. But if you place God at the center, balance will be restored, and your relationship will be sweeter, more favorable, and enduring.

Conclusion

Most women would argue that finding the right man is almost impossible, and it is true that dating and relationships can sometimes be hard. Yet finding the right man may not be as hard as you think. You may have to be a little more open-minded and be patient until you find the right man for you—or until he finds you.

Additionally, while most women complain that men are immature, not taking full responsibility in their lives, allowing a man to grow into himself advances not just personal growth but relationship growth as well. And though women often lament regarding men who they think of as too nice or as pushovers who do not stir any romantic feelings within them, giving a man his own space in the relationship while being the supportive woman in his life can make a man strive to do better.

Being the right woman for the right man also has a great impact on a lasting relationship. What this basically means is that when a woman compliments her man in most aspects of his life, he will be more receptive to bringing happiness to the table. Clearly, it goes to show that in every aspect of the relationship, there must be a give and take role for each so that the relationship flourishes.

Every woman needs to know that a man will be that good man to and for her when he sees his woman striving to be the best, supporting him, and making every effort to maintain the relationship. This will make the man strive for the better and bring out the best in him. Ultimately, a man just wants a woman who will be there through it all.

Printed in the United States
By Bookmasters